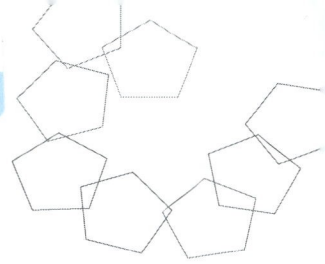

Foreword

The OECD's Directorate for Education helps member and non-member economies to foster human and social capital skills and leverage education and training systems to shape dynamic and sustainable futures. This means preparing learners for more rapid change than ever before. Key questions concern how skills can be matched to new needs, how to foster innovation, how to equip teachers for the 21st century, and how to reinforce the positive social impacts of education. We encourage countries to compare their performance and experience, and to learn from each other.

Education has been part of the OECD's work since the organisation was created 50 years ago but its importance over that time has grown markedly, both within countries' policy agendas and within the OECD itself. This growing prominence lay behind the decision to create a separate Directorate for Education in 2002. As reflected in this report's different chapters, we follow a "lifelong" approach to education and training. Our work also has a strong focus on quality and outcomes, equity, and innovation.

Knowledge management plays a key role in a world of information overload and knowledge-based economies. Traditionally, as OECD analyses have shown, education has not been exemplar in its own knowledge management, despite "knowledge" being education's core business. Given the significant volume of publications we produce each year, it is even more important that we provide a coherent overview of their key messages. This report aims to present the key findings and orientations for policy in an accessible way so that they can be used by different audiences – our own national contacts, other sections of governments, experts, media and the wider public – who do not have the time to stay abreast of all of the OECD's work on education. It is designed to encourage readers who know about only one or two of our studies to look further into those that they have been missing so far.

We have chosen to limit the scope of this report so that it includes only published results and policy orientations, and those applicable to most OECD countries (rather than, for example, single country reviews). The coverage is limited to work produced by the Directorate for Education, but it includes some analyses that have been conducted jointly with other OECD Directorates. A recent example is the OECD's horizontal "Innovation Strategy" to which the Directorate for Education made an important contribution regarding education and skills for innovation.

Education Today: The OECD Perspective is only one example of the priority we have been giving recently to weaving the different strands of the Directorate's analyses more closely together and to highlighting our main messages, in addition to our longstanding annual flagship publication *Education at a Glance*. As part of the new GPS programme which we are currently pursuing, we are establishing a knowledge management framework for our work on education, the integration of the evidence base from past and current analyses into this framework, and reinforcing the links between our education work programme and OECD's broader economic and social agenda. In 2009, we created an online collaborative space called *educationtoday* which offers relevant information, evidence and discussions on the impact of the crisis on education and related issues.

Judging from the positive response to the first edition of *Education Today: The OECD Perspective* published in March 2009, our plans are now to make this report a regular feature. Within the Directorate for Education, this synthesis has been undertaken by the Centre for Educational Research and Innovation (CERI) with the text prepared by David Istance. From the Indicators and Analysis Division, Elisabeth Villoutreix and Niccolina Clements were responsible for editing, layout and proofreading, while Corinne Heckmann, Eric Charbonnier and Bo Hansson provided the statistical graphics. Joanne Caddy and Cassandra Davis provided advice and co-ordination with the related dissemination activities within the Directorate.

Barbara Ischinger
Director, Directorate for Education

The Directorate for Education is part of the OECD Secretariat and contributes to the Organisation's commitment to building a stronger, cleaner and fairer world economy.

We provide comparative data and analysis on education policy making to help build efficient and effective educational systems, and improve learning outcomes. We provide a forum where governments, business, civil society and academia can share best practices and learn from one another.

Our statistics and indicators provide a strong evidence base for international comparisons of all aspects of education systems. Our policy analyses facilitate peer learning across countries as new policy options are explored and experiences compared. Our future-oriented educational research helps shape policy agendas by identifying upcoming issues while drawing upon the overall breadth of the OECD's policy work.

Table of Contents

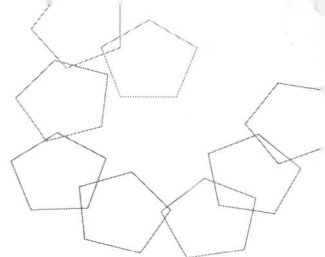

Introduction 9

▸ Chapter 1 ▪ **Early Childhood Education and Care** 11
    Introduction 12
    Key findings 12
    Policy directions 14

▸ Chapter 2 ▪ **Schooling – Investments, Organisation and Learners** 17
    Introduction 18
    Key findings 18
    Policy directions 24

▸ Chapter 3 ▪ **Transitions Beyond Initial Education** 29
    Introduction 30
    Key findings 30
    Policy directions 35

Chapter 4 ▪ **Higher Education** 39
    Introduction 40
    Key findings 40
    Policy directions 43

Chapter 5 ▪ **Lifelong Learning and Adults** 49
    Introduction 50
    Key findings 50
    Policy directions 52

▸ Chapter 6 ▪ **Outcomes, Benefits and Returns** 57
    Introduction 58
    Key findings 58
    Policy directions 64

Chapter 7 ▪ **Equity and Equality of Opportunity** 67
    Introduction 68
    Key findings 68
    Policy directions 73

▸ Chapter 8 ▪ **Innovation and Knowledge Management** 79
    Introduction 80
    Key findings 80
    Policy directions 83

BOXES

Box 3.1 ▪ Youth and economic crisis...33
Box 8.1 ▪ Innovation in education...81

FIGURES

Figure 1.1 ▪ Most children come into education well before the age of 5 years (2008).................13

Figure 2.1 ▪ Average class size in educational institutions, by level of education (2008).............19
Figure 2.2 ▪ Total number of intended instruction hours in public institutions between
the ages of 7 and 14 (2008)..21

Figure 3.1 ▪ Completion of upper secondary education is now the norm
across OECD countries (2008)...32

Figure 4.1 ▪ Population that has attained tertiary education (2008)..41
Figure 4.2 ▪ Distribution of foreign students in tertiary education,
by country of destination (2008)...43

Figure 5.1 ▪ Participation in formal and/or non-formal education,
by adults aged 25-64 years-old and educational attainment (2007).........................51

Figure 6.1 ▪ The spread of student proficiency levels in science in OECD countries (2006).........59
Figure 6.2 ▪ The spread of student proficiency levels in mathematics
in OECD countries (2006)..59
Figure 6.3 ▪ The spread of student proficiency levels in reading in OECD countries (2006).........60
Figure 6.4 ▪ Relative earnings from employment, by level of educational attainment
and gender for 25-64 year-olds (2008 or latest year available)................................62

Figure 7.1 ▪ Women have overtaken men in upper secondary and higher education:
Attainments of different adult age groups (2008)..69
Figure 7.2 ▪ Proportion of 20-24 year-olds who are not in education
and have not attained upper secondary education, by migrant status (2007).........71

This book has...

StatLinkS ▦▥▤
A service that delivers Excel® files
from the printed page!

Look for the *StatLinks* at the bottom left-hand corner of the tables or graphs in this book.
To download the matching Excel® spreadsheet, just type the link into your Internet browser,
starting with the *http://dx.doi.org* prefix.
If you're reading the PDF e-book edition, and your PC is connected to the Internet, simply
click on the link. You'll find *StatLinks* appearing in more OECD books.

Note on Country Coverage and Levels of Education

Country coverage

OECD and partner countries: The different sources from different dates used in this volume mean that OECD membership may not be identical in all cases. The entries cover the 33 countries that were members of the OECD when this report was drafted, as well as a number of partner countries and territories. Israel and Slovenia recently became members of the OECD and are therefore included in the list of OECD countries, but not in the calculation of OECD averages.

The statistical data for Israel are supplied by and under the responsibility of the relevant Israeli authorities. The use of such data by the OECD is without prejudice to the status of the Golan Heights, East Jerusalem and Israeli settlements in the West Bank under the terms of international law.

Levels of education

Education systems vary considerably from country to country, including the ages at which students typically begin and end each phase of schooling, the duration of courses, and what is taught. To facilitate the compilation of internationally comparable statistics on education, the United Nations created an International Standard Classification of Education (ISCED), which provides a basis for comparing different education systems and a standard terminology.

Readers should note that *Education Today* may use simplified terminology from that used in the ISCED classification and in *Education at a Glance 2010*.

Levels of education and ISCED classification

Pre-primary education/early childhood education ISCED 0
The first stage of organised education. Minimum entry age to pre-primary education is 3 years of age though "early childhood education and care" is not as restricted in terms of age or preparation for schooling.

Primary education ISCED 1
Designed to provide a sound basic education with entry age between 5 and 7 years of age. Duration tends to be 6 years.

Lower secondary education ISCED 2
Completes provision of basic education, usually with greater subject orientation. In some countries, the end of this level marks the end of compulsory education.

Upper secondary education ISCED 3
Even stronger subject specialisation than at lower secondary level, with teachers often more highly qualified. Students typically expected to have completed 9 years of education or lower secondary schooling before entry and are generally around the age of 15 or 16.

Post-secondary non-tertiary education ISCED 4
Programmes at this level may be regarded nationally as part of upper secondary or post-secondary education, but in terms of international comparison they are counted as post-secondary as entry typically requires completion of an upper secondary programme. Content may not be much more advanced than at upper secondary and is lower than at the tertiary level. Duration is usually equivalent to between 6 months and 2 years of full-time study.

Tertiary education ISCED 5 (sub-categories 5A and 5B)
ISCED 5 is the first stage of tertiary education. ISCED distinguishes between levels 5A (longer and more theoretical programmes) and 5B (programmes are shorter and more practically oriented). As tertiary education differs greatly between countries, the demarcation between these two sub-categories is not always clear cut.

Advanced research programmes ISCED 6
The second stage of tertiary education, devoted to advanced study and original research.

For fuller definitions and explanations of the ISCED standard, go to *www.unesco.org/education/information/nfsunesco/doc/isced_1997.htm.*

Introduction

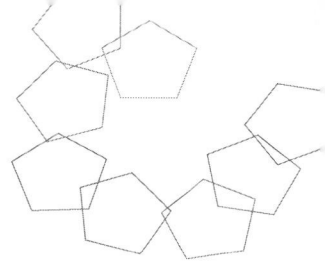

This summary report is based on results from OECD work produced since 2002 when the Directorate for Education was created, and especially in the past three to four years. The background to its preparation is explained in the Foreword by Director Barbara Ischinger. The approach chosen focuses on results and policy orientations which are published and hence in the public domain. Only generalised findings about developments, policy or practice relevant across most OECD countries have been included. So, not covered are: studies or reviews of single countries; publications which provide exchange of information on promising practice without broader analytical conclusions; work plans and programme intentions; and clarifying statements of problems, challenges or issues.

It is divided into eight chapters, devised as a structure to reflect well the different areas of educational work and to bring out policy conclusions and messages. It is produced entirely in modular format rather than as a continuous narrative. Each of the sections is divided into, respectively, *Introduction, Key Findings* and *Policy Directions*. Each modular text is introduced by the key message it contains or, where the module is in the form of a list of messages, these are highlighted instead. Each text also includes the title and chapter reference to the OECD report from which it comes, and these titles are brought together in a bibliography at the end of each chapter. A selection of illustrative figures and boxes has also been included to complement the text. This report uses the OECD's *StatLinks* service and below each table and figure is a stable URL.

In reporting findings and conclusions, the volume avoids reference to specific projects, organisational units and internal structures within the Directorate for Education as these are largely uninteresting to the external audience. The introductions to each chapter do, however, make some connection to particular projects and future plans as an additional signpost for linking outcomes and messages to the work being undertaken.

In order to stay within manageable limits, this resource is highly selective of all the possible findings and policy orientations regarding education at the OECD. As the included texts are removed from the fuller analyses from which they are taken, there is a natural risk of over-simplification with short conclusions taken out of their wider analytical context. For both of these reasons, therefore, it is strongly advised that users looking for more than the headline messages should refer back to the original OECD source for the fuller picture.

1

Early Childhood Education and Care

Participation in education by three- and four-year-olds tends now to be high, though coverage is a third or less of the age group in several OECD countries. Early childhood education and care (ECEC) has been a growing priority in OECD countries, and the subject of past and ongoing OECD analysis. A major OECD review was published in 2006 – Starting Strong II: Early Childhood Education and Care, from which many of these conclusions are drawn – which has been followed up with an ongoing international network. There are wide differences between systems, including between those which have a strong "preparation for school" approach and those implementing a broader social pedagogy, between those with mainly public provision and those relying strongly on private household resources, as well as in the relative emphasis on education and childcare. Improving the quality of ECEC is a universal issue, as is enhancing the contribution of ECEC to equity.

INTRODUCTION

Early childhood provision – pre-primary and childcare – has been a growing priority in many countries. Such priority is manifest by demanding parents, who tend more and more to be both employed while their children are young. It is also a phase of education and services increasingly recognised as important in its contribution to a wide range of social, economic and educational goals. At the same time, it is a sector with a complex diversity of players and partners, and one with a significant lack of investment in many countries.

A major OECD review in the field of early childhood – *Starting Strong II: Early Childhood Education and Care,* published in 2006 – was a follow-up to an earlier international review published in 2001. Its policy orientations are broadly focused on overcoming the under-developed status of the sector that remains typical of many countries. The Starting Strong Network has continued since then to help countries to develop effective and efficient approaches, and good practice in the field of early childhood education and care (ECEC). It does so through its clearing house of new policy research, data and methodology development, workshops, and by fostering contacts among professionals worldwide.

In future, policy work on "Encouraging Quality in Early Childhood Education and Care" will investigate what defines quality, which policies can promote and enhance quality, and how such policies can be effectively put in place. It will focus in particular on the challenge of moving from policy analysis to successful implementation. Our work also focuses on raising the quality of the workforce in early childhood education and care, as well as integrating early learning with broader social policies and the needs of working parents.

KEY FINDINGS

In the majority of countries – but not all – education now begins for most well before 5 years old: Already over two-thirds of the age group of young children aged 3 and 4 years (71.5%) are enrolled in education across OECD countries as a whole, and this rises to nearly 80% (79.8%) in the OECD countries that are part of the European Union. Enrolment rates for early childhood education at this age range from over 90% in Belgium, Denmark, France, Germany, Iceland, Italy, New Zealand, Norway, Spain, Sweden and the United Kingdom, at one end of the spectrum, to less than a third in Australia, Greece, Korea, Switzerland and Turkey.
📖 *Education at a Glance 2010: OECD Indicators,* 2010, Indicator C1

Demand for early childhood provision for those aged under 3 years far outstrips supply in all but the Nordic region: The highest levels of enrolment of infants less than 3 years of age in early childhood education and care in publicly-subsidised provision are found in Denmark and Sweden. Apart from these two countries and Finland, the evidence of OECD reviews shows that the demand for services for young children is significantly higher than the places available, even in countries with provision for long parental leave. In countries where public funding for such provision is limited, most working parents must either seek solutions in the private market, where ability to pay significantly influences accessibility to quality services, or else rely on informal arrangements with family, friends and neighbours. The publicly-subsidised services for these young children take several forms: family day care, centre-based *crèche* services and integrated services.
📖 *Starting Strong II: Early Childhood Education and Care,* 2006, Chapter 4

Figure 1.1.

Most children come into education well before the age of 5 years (2008)

Children aged 4 years and younger as a percentage of 3- and 4-year-olds
Full-time and part-time students in public and private institutions

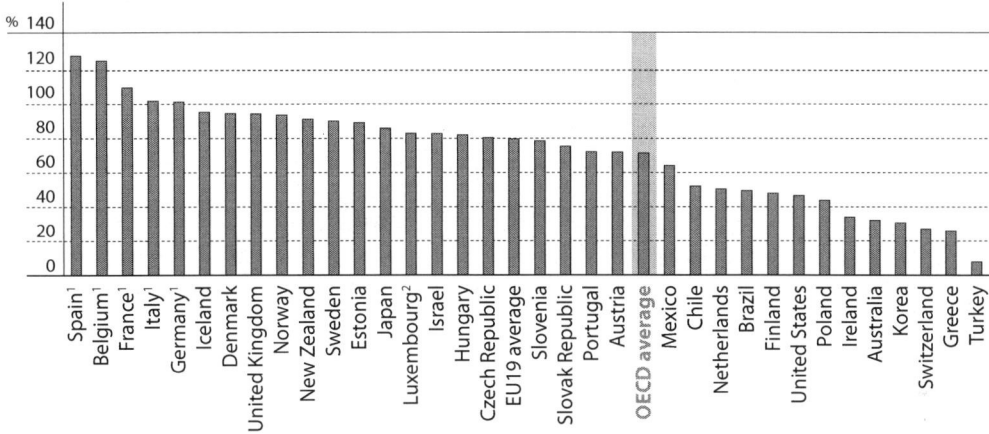

1. The rates "4 years and younger as a percentage of 3- and 4-year-olds" include a significant number of children under 3 years of age; the net rates between ages 3 and 5 are around 100%.
2. Underestimated because many resident children are in provision in neighbouring countries.
Source: OECD (2010), *Education at a Glance 2010: OECD Indicators*, OECD Publishing.

StatLink ▨◧▨ http://dx.doi.org/10.1787/888932310415

Publicly-funded pre-primary provision tends to be more strongly developed in the European than in the non-European countries of the OECD: In Europe, the concept of universal access of 3- to 6-year-olds is generally accepted. Most countries in this region provide all children with at least two years of free, publicly-funded provision before they begin primary provision. With the exception of Ireland and the Netherlands, such access is generally a statutory right from the age of 3 years and in some even before that. Early education programmes in Europe are often free and attached to schools. In OECD countries outside Europe, free early education tends to be only available from age 5, though many children are enrolled from age 4 in Australia, Korea and some US states.
📖 *Starting Strong II: Early Childhood Education and Care*, 2006, Chapter 4

Two broad emphases in early education characterise different countries – preparing for school and social pedagogy: OECD countries approach the partnership between early childhood services and the primary school in different ways – all trying to improve the co-ordination between the sectors but starting from different premises. Broadly, there are two different approaches across countries. France and the English-speaking countries tend to see the question of partnership from the point of view of the school: early education should serve the objectives of public education and provide children with "readiness for school" skills. In contrast, countries inheriting the social pedagogy tradition (the Nordic and Central European countries) see kindergarten as a specific institution turned more to supporting families and the broad development needs of young children.
📖 *Starting Strong II: Early Childhood Education and Care*, 2006, Chapter 3

A positive consequence of decentralisation has been the integration of early childhood education and care services at the local level, leading to a more efficient allocation of resources to children: New services tend to be less bound by traditional competency boundaries than government departments. Many local authorities in Austria, Denmark, Finland, France, Hungary, Germany, Italy, the Netherlands, Norway, Sweden, the United Kingdom and the United States have brought together children's services and education portfolios to plan more effectively and provide coherence of services for young children and their families. Some local authorities have integrated administration and policy development across age groups and sectors: in Denmark, Italy, Norway, Sweden and the United Kingdom, for example, an increasing number of local authorities have reorganised responsibility for early childhood education and care, and for schools (and sometimes other children's services) under one administrative department and political committee.

📖 *Starting Strong II: Early Childhood Education and Care,* 2006, Chapter 2

The devolution of powers and responsibilities can, however, also widen differences of access and quality between states, regions or districts: This has occurred in Sweden but is even more evident in federal countries such as Australia, Canada, Germany and the United States, where unified national policies have been difficult to achieve. Unless strong equalising mechanisms are in place, decentralised early childhood administrations in poor urban areas can also face difficulties because of low taxation revenues. Decentralisation and well-intentioned policies in some countries (*e.g.* Canada and Hungary) have led to the creation of independent rural areas which are too small or too poor to support quality early childhood education and care services without strong state assistance. Even in situations where funding is available (such as in Australia), effective co-ordination can be inhibited by a highly dispersed population, separate state auspices for pre-school education, and a market-oriented approach to childcare.

📖 *Starting Strong II: Early Childhood Education and Care,* 2006, Chapter 2

Disabled children and those with learning and behavioural difficulties receive less additional support at the pre-primary than at the primary level: The median percentage of the children at pre-primary level receiving additional financial resources specifically for "disabilities" was 1.1% in 2003 – significantly lower than for children at the primary level (3.6%), though there are examples (*e.g.* the United States) of free early childhood education for disabled children. The median percentage of children in pre-primary education receiving additional resources for "learning and behavioural difficulties" is even lower at 0.3% for the countries reporting data in 2003, again with some notable exceptions (*e.g.* England [9.6%] and Chile [11.5%]). The percentage of children receiving additional resources because of "social disadvantages" was negligible in many countries; in this case, the exceptions were Belgium (French Community) and Mexico with 12.9% and 16.0%, respectively.

📖 *Students with Disabilities, Learning Difficulties and Disadvantages: Policies, Statistics and Indicators – 2007 Edition,* 2008, Chapter 4

POLICY DIRECTIONS

Early childhood education and care policy needs to be systemic and integrate the different forms of early childhood provision, allow universal access, and enjoy a strong and equal partnership with the rest of the education system. The OECD review of this sector proposes ten policy areas for consideration:

- **Place well-being, early development and learning at the core of early childhood approaches:** Rather than being an adjunct to labour market policies with weak development agendas or an under-resourced "Cinderella" education service, early childhood education and care needs to have the child and her/his well-being and learning at the core.

- **Aspire towards early childhood education and care systems that support broad learning, participation and democracy:** The touchstones of a democratic approach are to extend the agency of the child and right of parents to be involved in the education of their children. Learning to be, learning to do, learning to learn, and learning to live together are the critical elements to be promoted in each child.

- **Provide autonomy, funding and support to early childhood services:** Within the parameters of system-wide goals and guidelines, educators and services should have the autonomy to plan and to choose curricula for the children in their care; policy should provide the means for staff to exercise such autonomy and participatory approaches.

- **Develop with the stakeholders broad guidelines and curricular standards for all early childhood education and care services:** Guiding frameworks – especially when they have been developed together by the key stakeholders – help to promote a more even quality across early childhood provision, to guide and support professional staff, and to facilitate communication between staff and families.

- **Base public funding on achieving quality pedagogical goals:** Most countries need to double their annual investment per child to ensure child-staff ratios and qualified staff on some parity with the primary sector; the investment should be directed to achieving quality pedagogical goals rather than simply aiming to create sufficient places.

- **Improve the working conditions and professional education of early childhood education and care staff:** The OECD reviews found a number of common weaknesses that need attention. These are: low recruitment and pay levels, particularly in child care services; lack of certification in specialist early childhood pedagogy; excessive feminisation of staff; and lack of diversity of staff to reflect neighbourhood diversity.

- **Create the governance structures necessary for system accountability and quality assurance:** These include such elements as strong expert policy units, data collection and monitoring capacity, an evaluation agency, and a pedagogical advisory or inspection corps.

- **Attend to the social context of early childhood development:** Well-organised services should work towards a broad but realistic vision to which the other stakeholders can subscribe, serving at the same time to support parents in child-rearing, facilitate women working, and help social inclusion for low-income and immigrant families.

- **Encourage family and community involvement in early childhood services:** The continuity of children's experience across the different early childhood education and care environments is greatly enhanced when parents and staff members share information and adopt consistent approaches to socialisation, daily routines, child development and learning; communities are important both as providers and as offering space for partnerships.

- **Reduce child poverty and exclusion through fiscal, social and labour policies, and increase resources for children with additional learning rights within universal programmes:** Research indicates the effectiveness of universal programmes for children with different disabilities and disadvantages, combined with enhanced funding and investment in quality services, rather than targeted programmes which serve to segregate and stigmatise.

📖 *Starting Strong II: Early Childhood Education and Care*, 2006, Chapter 10

References

OECD (2006), *Starting Strong II: Early Childhood Education and Care*, OECD Publishing.

OECD (2008), *Students with Disabilities, Learning Difficulties and Disadvantages: Policies, Statistics and Indicators – 2007 Edition*, OECD Publishing.

OECD (2010), *Education at a Glance 2010: OECD Indicators*, OECD Publishing.

2

SCHOOLING – INVESTMENTS, ORGANISATION AND LEARNERS

There have been major investments in schooling across OECD countries, including in teacher salaries. Shared patterns exist alongside notable differences such as in teacher beliefs (as charted with the Teaching and Learning International Survey [TALIS]) and in school time use. Since the 2005 study, Teachers Matter, *much OECD work has analysed the characteristics of learners and learning, teachers, and how to improve school leadership. Data from the Programme for International Student Assessment (PISA) have permitted specific analyses of aspects of schooling, such as student attitudes towards and knowledge of the environment. Work on the educational role of technology has shown how important is home use for educational outcomes. Policy orientations on schooling have stressed the need to professionalise and innovate, calling for reforms directed at effective learning to be placed at the core of schooling, rather than changing only structures and administrative systems. The OECD continues to analyse and stress the value of good school design and safe buildings.*

INTRODUCTION

The period of compulsory education – primary, lower secondary and even the upper secondary cycle in some countries – is at the core of all education systems. Over recent years, there have been significant investments in this core phase of education, recognised as fundamental for laying the foundation on which so many other social, economic and educational outcomes may follow. Teachers (and the educational workforce in general) are widely recognised as central to the success of schooling, a position reinforced by the major 2005 OECD study, *Teachers Matter: Attracting, Developing and Retaining Effective Teachers*.

OECD work has since then analysed with growing precision the characteristics of learners, teachers and the nature of school practices, including leadership. Policy orientations have stressed the need simultaneously to modernise, professionalise and innovate, while also placing reforms directed at effective learning – rather than changing only structures and administrative systems – at the core of schooling.

The Teaching and Learning International Survey (TALIS) was based on the experience of some 90 000 teachers and school principals, representing over 2 million professionals in 23 countries; first results were published in 2009. The OECD's triennial Programme for International Student Assessment (PISA) surveys have permitted focused analyses of schooling, ranging from the attitudes and awareness of students, through features of the learning environment, to the allocation of resources. The work of the Centre for Educational Research and Innovation (CERI) on, for instance, learning sciences and on the use of technology in education has offered a complementary set of international studies on aspects of schooling. *Improving School Leadership* has provided in-depth analyses of different approaches to school leadership as well as practical guidelines for improvement. The Centre for Effective Learning Environments (CELE) has continued to identify how best to design and deliver safe, healthy and high quality educational facilities.

KEY FINDINGS

Only a small minority of students do not now complete compulsory education overall, though rising to one-in-ten in some countries: The participation rates in most OECD and partner countries tend to be high until the end of compulsory education, with more than 90% completing this phase in most. Those where more than 10% do not complete this phase of education are: Belgium, Chile, Germany, Hungary, Mexico, the Netherlands, New Zealand, Turkey and the United States. The age which marks the end of compulsory attendance does vary, however, and in six of these cases is as late as 17 or 18 years of age (Belgium, Chile, Germany, Hungary, the Netherlands and the United States).
📖 *Education at a Glance 2010: OECD Indicators*, 2010, Indicator C1

Spending per student in schooling (plus post-secondary non-tertiary) has increased everywhere in OECD countries since the mid-1990s, contrasting with a mixed picture in tertiary education: Using 100 as the index for spending per school student in 2000, this indicator of change had risen to 125 by 2007 in OECD countries, well up from the OECD average 88 in 1995. (This compares with 114 for spending per tertiary education student in 2007 compared with 2000 levels, with the index falling over this time in several countries.) Even in only the short period since 2000, the rise in spending per school student was very marked in some countries, with the index reaching 152 in the Czech Republic, 171 in Hungary, 163 in Ireland, 161 in Korea, 168 in the Slovak Republic and 156 in the United Kingdom and, among parter countries, 186 in Estonia and 182 in Brazil. Only in Italy was the recent per school student spending level lower than in 2000 (and then marginally at 99).
📖 *Education at a Glance 2010: OECD Indicators*, 2010, Indicator B1

Classes are larger in lower secondary compared with primary schools (on average, just over two students more per class), alongside marked differences between countries with big and small classes: Lower secondary average class sizes of 30 or more in Chile, Israel, Japan and Korea contrast sharply with Denmark, Iceland, Luxembourg, and the partner country the Russian Federation where both primary and lower secondary classes are, on average, at or below 20 students per class. Primary school classes (21.6 per class OECD average) are generally smaller than in lower secondary schools (23.9 per class). There are minor exceptions to the "primary school classes are smaller" finding, but the most marked is the United Kingdom, with average primary class size of 24.6 compared with 20.4 at the lower secondary level.

📖 *Education at a Glance 2010: OECD Indicators*, 2010, Indicator D2

Figure 2.1.

Average class size in educational institutions, by level of education (2008)

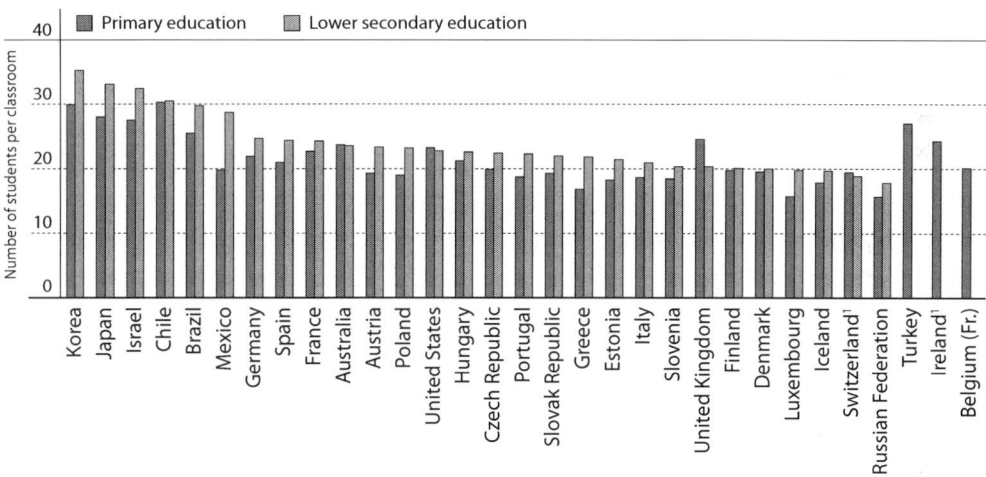

1. Public institutions only.
Source: OECD (2010), *Education at a Glance 2010: OECD Indicators*, OECD Publishing.

StatLink 🔗 http://dx.doi.org/10.1787/888932310491

The investments made in teachers, as indicated by teacher salary levels, have gone up in real terms over the past decade in most countries: Teachers' salaries have risen in real terms in both primary and secondary education in most of the countries for which the OECD has trends data (comparing 1996 and 2008 in 22 systems covering 20 countries). The biggest increases – approximately doubling – have taken place in Hungary and the partner country Estonia, in both where teacher salaries have been and remain relatively low. More generally, the increases have tended to be largest in those systems with still relatively low teacher salaries. Largely static or even falling salary levels are only found – but note that not all countries supply data on teacher salaries – for experienced teachers in Australia, lower and upper secondary teachers in the French Community of Belgium, top salaried teachers in Japan, starting teachers in Norway, teachers at the experienced levels in Spain, and starting primary teachers and those with 15 years of experience in Switzerland.

📖 *Education at a Glance 2010: OECD Indicators*, 2010, Indicator D3

Some countries use a "career-based" model of teacher employment and others a "position-based" model, each with its own strengths and weaknesses: In "career-based" systems, teachers expect to stay long in the public service after early entry and once recruited are allocated to posts according to internal rules (*e.g.* France, Japan, Korea and Spain). These systems tend to avoid problems of teacher shortages but with concerns about how far teacher education is connected to school and student needs, and with lack of incentives for continued professional development and of responsiveness to local needs. "Position-based" systems instead tend to select the "best" candidate for each position, whether by external recruitment or internal promotion, with wider access to the profession in terms of age or previous career experience (*e.g.* Canada, Sweden, Switzerland and the United Kingdom). The problems typically encountered in these systems are shortages, especially in mathematics, sciences, etc., difficulties in ensuring a core of good older teachers, and wider teacher quality gaps between attractive and unattractive districts/schools.

📖 *Teachers Matter: Attracting, Developing and Retaining Effective Teachers*, 2005, Executive Summary

Substantial differences exist between countries in teacher beliefs about how teaching should be delivered: In most countries teachers see their job as helping students actively to develop and construct their knowledge rather than concentrate on transmitting content only (among the TALIS countries, the exception is Italy where only a minority endorses this view). Whereas a clear majority of teachers support a constructivist approach in Australia, Korea, North-Western Europe and Scandinavia, belief in direct transmission is much more in evidence in Malaysia, South America and Southern Europe. Teachers in Eastern Europe lie in between in the balance of teachers having mainly constructivist or mainly transmission beliefs.

📖 *Creating Effective Teaching and Learning Environments: First Results from TALIS,* 2009, Chapter 4 and Executive Summary

Teachers are positive about the appraisal and feedback they receive, but in some countries a significant minority or even majority of teachers have not received any in recent years: Teachers across the different systems surveyed by TALIS tend to be positive about the appraisal and feedback they receive, reporting that on the whole it is fair and helpful for their work, and increases their job satisfaction. Approximately 13% of teachers surveyed by TALIS reported that they had received no feedback or evaluation in their current school in the previous five years; this average level rises to much higher levels in Ireland (26%), Italy (55%), Portugal (26%) and Spain (46%).

📖 *Creating Effective Teaching and Learning Environments: First Results from TALIS* 2009, Chapter 5 and Executive Summary

High proportions of lower secondary teachers participate in professional development but many say that they would like more: Nearly 9 teachers in 10 surveyed by TALIS reported having taken part in a structured professional development activity in the preceding 18 months, though in Denmark, the Slovak Republic and Turkey around a quarter reported no participation during that period. Despite generally high levels of participation, more than half the teachers (55%) in the TALIS countries overall say that they would have liked more professional development, and lack of suitable opportunities is a significant factor in this. Approximately a third of the surveyed teachers reported a high level of need for training to help them teach students with special learning needs. Other professional development priorities include teaching with ICT and dealing with difficult student behaviour.

📖 *Creating Effective Teaching and Learning Environments: First Results from TALIS*, 2009, Chapter 3 and Executive Summary

Figure 2.2.

Total number of intended instruction hours in public institutions between the ages of 7 and 14 (2008)

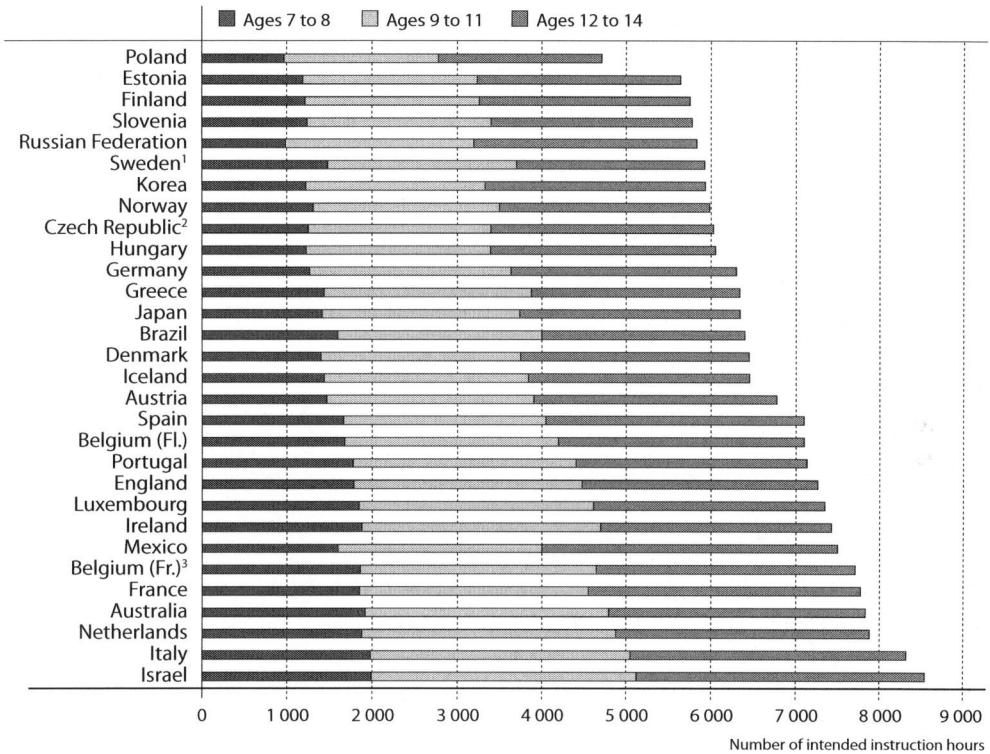

■ Ages 7 to 8   ☐ Ages 9 to 11   ▓ Ages 12 to 14

Number of intended instruction hours

1. Estimated because breakdown by age not available.
2. Minimum number of hours per year.
3. "Ages 12-14" covers ages 12-13 only.
Source: OECD (2010), *Education at a Glance 2010: OECD Indicators*, OECD Publishing.

StatLink ᴍᴤ🔳 http://dx.doi.org/10.1787/888932310472

High "intended instruction hours" for those in school between the ages of 7 and 14 years-old bear no obvious association with higher academic performance at age 15: The average for OECD countries in "intended instruction hours" added up from requirements regarding students between the ages of 7 and 14 years is 6 777 hours, the large majority of which are compulsory. This covers the compulsory and non-compulsory time when schools must offer teaching to school students (actual hours may vary even widely from this, with variations too by region or type of school). Requirements vary very widely among OECD countries, from 4 715 in Poland to 8 316 in Italy, and higher still at 8 541 hours in Israel (Poland thus requires barely over half of intended instruction time [55%] compared with Israel, and only 57% compared with Italy). Poland has seen notable increases in PISA scores, and two countries that achieve particularly well – Finland and Korea – also have relatively low intended hours at 5 752 and 5 934, respectively.

📖 *Education at a Glance 2010: OECD Indicators*, 2010, Indicator D1

High performance tends to be associated with high relative time in regular lessons and moderate absolute time: The relative balance spent in regular as opposed to out-of-school learning seems to be particularly influential. In high-performing countries, the largest proportion of students' learning time (70% to 80%) happens within regular school lessons, whereas in low-performing countries, half or more of students' learning time occurs outside regular lessons. Longer hours do not by themselves bestow an advantage as in many countries long hours in regular mathematics lessons is actually associated with lower performance compared with moderate hours. As exceptions, in Korea and the partner economies Chinese Taipei and Hong Kong-China, those spending long hours learning mathematics in regular lessons perform significantly better in this subject than other students.

📖 *Quality Time for Students: Learning In and Out of School*, forthcoming, Chapter 4

School leadership is pivotal for the quality of schooling through creating the right organisational and educational conditions for effectiveness and improvement: A large body of research evidence on school effectiveness and improvement consistently highlights the pivotal role of leadership. It is nevertheless a complex role as leaders largely work outside the classrooms where the teaching and learning takes place. Hence, instead of shaping quality directly, leaders do so by creating the right conditions for good teaching and learning through such factors as professional motivations, capacities and working environments. They are especially influential as regards four key dimensions: improving teacher quality; goal-setting, assessment and accountability; strategic resource management; and collaboration with external partners.

📖 *Improving School Leadership: Volume 1: Policy and Practice*, 2008, Chapter 1

PISA data permit the analysis of computer use in schools and at home, and how these relate to educational performance. Based on the 2006 survey data, some key findings to emerge are:

- **All students in OECD countries are now familiar with computers:** less than 1% of 15-year-old students in OECD countries declared that they had never used a computer.

- **Frequent use of computers at home is not matched by equivalent use at school:** The OECD average for 15-year-olds reporting frequently using computers at home is 86%, compared with only 55% reporting their frequent use in school. Exceptionally in Hungary, frequent school use (86%) actually exceeds frequent home use (85%), albeit by a narrow margin.

- **There is a stronger correlation between educational performance and computer use at home than with its use in school:** In most countries, the benefits of greater computer use at home tend to be larger than its use at school. In every country, students reporting "rare" or "no use" of computers at home score lower than their counterparts who report frequent use. But in school, more intensive computer use is not associated with better results.

📖 *Are the New Millennium Learners Making the Grade? Technology Use and Educational Performance in PISA*, 2010, Chapter 5 and Executive Summary

Some countries persist with repetition of school years as common practice despite its cost – to individuals and the system alike: In some school systems (France, Luxembourg and Spain), up to one-quarter of lower secondary school students repeat a year at some point, as do over 20% of primary pupils in the Netherlands and Mexico. But this is not the common situation across OECD countries. Although year repetition is often popular with teachers, there is little evidence that children gain benefit from it. Repetition is expensive – the full economic cost is up to USD 20 000 equivalent for each student who repeats a year – and schools have few incentives to take into account the costs involved.

📖 *No More Failures: Ten Steps to Equity in Education*, 2007, Chapter 4

Leading researchers from Europe and North America have summarised large bodies of research on learning in such a way as to be relevant to educational leaders and policy makers. The transversal conclusions that emerge suggest that to be most effective a learning environment should fit the following "principles" and that ideally all should be present:

- **Recognise the learners as its core participants,** encourage their active engagement and develop in them an understanding of their own activity as learners.
- **Be founded on the social nature of learning** and actively encourage well-organised co-operative learning.
- Be where the learning professionals are highly **attuned to the learners' motivations and the key role of emotions** in achievement.
- **Be acutely sensitive to the individual differences** among the learners in it, including their prior knowledge.
- Devise programme that demand **hard work and challenge from all without excessive overload.**
- Operate with clarity of expectations, **use assessment strategies consistent with these expectations,** and give strong emphasis on formative feedback.
- **Strongly promote "horizontal connectedness"** across areas of knowledge and subjects, as well as to the community and the wider world.

📖 *The Nature of Learning: Using Research to Inspire Practice*, 2010, Chapter 13 and Executive Summary

Students are generally positive about school as a place, with younger and more successful students and girls the more positive: The evidence on student attitudes, from diverse international and national sources, reveals several general tendencies on reported satisfaction: students are fairly satisfied with school in general, although older students less than younger ones; students in higher tracks are more positive than students in lower tracks; and girls tend to be more positive about school than boys. Countries where the measured sense of belonging is lowest among 15-year-olds are the Czech Republic, France, Belgium and Japan, and especially Korea and Poland. The cases of Japan and Korea show that low engagement can go hand in hand with high achievement. Countries where engagement is highest are Sweden, Ireland, Hungary and the United Kingdom.

📖 *Demand-sensitive Schooling? Evidence and Issues*, 2006; *Student Engagement at School: A Sense of Belonging and Participation: Results from PISA 2000*, 2003

Immigrant students are motivated learners and have positive attitudes towards school: Immigrant students report similar or even higher levels of positive learning dispositions compared with their native peers. First generation and second generation students often report higher levels of interest and motivation in mathematics, and more positive attitudes towards schooling than native-born students, and in none of the countries do immigrant students report lower levels on these engagement and interest indicators. The consistency of this finding is striking given that there are substantial differences between countries in terms of immigrant populations, policies and histories, as well as immigrant student performance in PISA 2003.

📖 *Where Immigrant Students Succeed: A Comparative Review of Performance and Engagement in PISA 2003*, 2006, Chapter 4

Fifteen-year-olds across the world report their strong interest in environmental issues and identify their schooling as the most important source of knowledge about the environment: Students across the world report their strong interest in issues related to the environment. They also cite school – particularly but not only in their geography and science lessons – as the place where they learn most

about the environment. Student awareness of environmental issues tends to go hand in hand with their measured level of scientific knowledge and proficiency. On the other hand, those with lower proficiency levels in environmental science tend to be more optimistic that the environment will improve in the future highlighting the important role that education can play in raising awareness.

📖 *Green at Fifteen? How 15-Year-Olds Perform in Environmental Science and Geoscience in PISA 2006*, 2009, Chapters 3 and 4

Certain countries strongly maintain the public nature of schooling by accepting neither private provision nor homeschooling: Most OECD countries report that independent (not government-dependent) private schools are permitted in their system, even if the number of students involved is usually relatively small. However, they are not permitted in the Czech Republic, Finland, the Slovak Republic and Sweden, and for the lower secondary level in Korea, too. Homeschooling is also an option in many countries, albeit under certain conditions, but is not allowed in Germany, Greece, Japan, Korea, Mexico, Spain and partner country Brazil, and not at the lower secondary level in the Czech and Slovak Republics.

📖 *Education at a Glance 2010: OECD Indicators*, 2010, Indicator D5

The closer parents are to schooling provision, the more satisfied they tend to be about its achievements: Parents tend to be more satisfied with their own children's school than with the state of education in general; parents with children in school more satisfied than other parents; those involved in school governance more than other parents; women – who tend to be more active in their children's education and the life of the school – more than men. In evidence from diverse national studies, there is a generally positive level of reported satisfaction with schools by parents and the public. Education appears to be a high public priority, alongside health, and higher than many other calls on the public purse.

📖 *Demand-sensitive Schooling? Evidence and Issues*, 2006, Chapter 2

POLICY DIRECTIONS

Teacher employment and deployment are organised along markedly different lines in different systems: in some this follows a "career-based" model; in others, a "position-based" model. OECD analysis proposes the following directions to inform policy development whichever of the two applies:

- **Emphasise teacher quality over teacher quantity:** There is substantial research indicating that the quality of teachers and their teaching is the most important factor shaping student outcomes that is open to significant policy influence. Key ingredients in the teacher quality agenda include: more attention to the criteria for selection into initial teacher education and employment; ongoing evaluation throughout the career to identify areas for improvement; and recognising and rewarding effective practice.

- **Develop teacher profiles to align teacher development and performance with school needs:** Countries need to have clear, concise statements of what teachers are expected to know and be able to do; these need to be embedded throughout the school and teacher education systems. The teacher profiles should encompass strong subject matter knowledge, pedagogical skills, the capacity to work effectively with a wide range of students and colleagues, to contribute to the school and the profession, and the capacity to continue developing.

- **View teacher development as a continuum:** The stages of initial teacher education, induction and professional development need to be well connected to create a coherent learning and development system for teachers – which they tend not to be in most countries. Lifelong learning for teachers implies supporting them more effectively in the early career stages and then in providing incentives and resources for ongoing professional development.

- **Make teacher education and entry more flexible:** Provide more routes into the profession including: post-graduate study following an initial qualification in a subject matter field; para-professionals and teacher's aides given opportunities to gain full qualifications; and mid-career changers able to combine reduced teaching loads and concurrent participation in teacher preparation.

- **Transform teaching into a knowledge-rich profession:** Teachers need to be active agents in analysing their own practice in the light of professional standards and their own students' learning. Teachers need to engage more actively with new knowledge and with professional development focused on the evidence base of improved practice.

- **Provide schools with genuine responsibility for teacher personnel management:** The evidence suggests that too often the selection process is dominated by rules about qualifications and seniority that bear little relationship to the qualifications needed to be an effective teacher. The school is the key agency for student learning – and hence for teacher selection, development, etc. – but will need highly-skilled leadership teams and support to carry this out.

📖 *Teachers Matter: Attracting, Developing and Retaining Effective Teachers*, 2005, Executive Summary

The quality of school leadership needs to be enhanced and it needs to be made sustainable. Four main policy levers, taken together, can improve school leadership practice:

- **Redefine school leadership responsibilities:** Leaders need to exercise a significant degree of autonomy if they are to influence quality, and policy should ensure that they have this. Policy should encourage leaders to: support, evaluate and develop teacher quality; engage in goal-setting and organisational evaluation; enhance strategic financial and human resource management; and operate more widely than within the confines of the school itself.

- **Distribute school leadership:** Leadership is strengthened, not weakened, if the responsibilities of school principals are shared effectively with other middle management and school professionals, and with school boards; policy should support and enable this to happen.

- **Develop skills for effective school leadership:** School leadership demands specific advanced competences that explicitly need development. Leadership development should contribute to the different career stages so policies should distinguish between preparation for leadership, induction programmes, and adequate in-service opportunities adapted to need and context. This career focus will also enhance attractiveness (next point).

- **Make school leadership an attractive profession:** Ensuring that the procedures for recruiting the key personnel of school leadership are highly professionalised is one important route to enhancing attractiveness. Another is to establish salaries at levels commensurate with workloads and responsibilities, compared with classroom teachers and those in other professions, and linked to local factors which influence attractiveness.

📖 *Improving School Leadership: Volume 1: Policy and Practice,* 2008, Executive Summary; *Improving School Leadership: Volume 3: The Toolkit,* 2010

The recent analysis of educational technology use by 15-year-olds and its relationship to achievement levels resulted in a number of policy recommendations . These include:

- **Raise awareness among educators, parents and policy makers of the consequences of increasing ICT familiarity:** Policy makers should recognise that students need technology and access to digital media for learning in 21st century societies. Teachers and the teacher education sector need to hear this clear policy message, as do parents that they also have a crucial responsibility in developing responsible attitudes to using digital media.

- **Identify and foster the development of 21st century skills and competences:** The skills and competences required by a knowledge economy are either supported or enhanced by ICT. Policy authorities should identify and conceptualise the required competence set so as to incorporate them into the educational standards that students should meet by the end of compulsory schooling.

- **Adopt holistic policy approaches to ICT in education:** Many countries have not developed holistic policies for the educational use of ICT. An overall favourable environment, the inclusion of ICT in curriculum design, and strong leadership and commitment from teachers and principals to implement ICT-rich teaching all significantly influence the use of ICT in schools. Current policies and their results should be critically evaluated within such a holistic framework.

- **Adapt school learning environments as computer ratios improve and digital learning resources increase:** Students should be able to locate and use a computer at any time, depending on their specific individual and team assignments. Governments should provide the conditions for innovations to flourish and should assess their effects.

- **Promote greater computer use at school and experimental research on its effects:** The positive gains from computer use at home derive in part because its frequency has passed a critical threshold; it is far above the relatively marginal use often experienced at school. Governments need to create the necessary incentives for teachers to engage with ICT sufficiently that its benefits can be realised, and they should support the creation of the evidence base of "what works".

📖 *Are the New Millennium Learners Making the Grade? Technology Use and Educational Performance in PISA*, 2010, Chapter 5 and Executive Summary

Seismic safety in schools should be recognised as an important goal and national programmes should be established on an urgent basis to assure earthquake safety of new and existing schools. The principles guiding such programmes should include:

- **Establish clear and measurable objectives for school seismic safety,** based on the level of risk which can be implemented and supported by the affected residents of communities and agencies at the local government level.

- **Define the level of the earthquake hazard** in order to facilitate the development and application of construction codes and standards.

- **Specify the desired ability of school buildings to resist earthquakes.** School buildings should be designed and constructed or retrofitted to prevent collapse, partial collapse or other failure that would endanger human life when subjected to specified levels of ground shaking and/or collateral seismic hazards.

- **Give priority to making new schools safe.** A longer timeframe will likely be needed to correct seismic weaknesses of existing school buildings.

📖 *OECD Recommendations Concerning Guidelines on Earthquake Safety in Schools*, 2005; *School Safety and Security: Keeping Schools Safe in Earthquakes*, 2004

References

OECD (2003), *Student Engagement at School: A Sense of Belonging and Participation: Results from PISA 2000*, OECD Publishing.

OECD (2004), *School Safety and Security: Keeping Schools Safe in Earthquakes*, OECD Publishing.

OECD (2005), *Teachers Matter: Attracting, Developing and Retaining Effective Teachers*, OECD Publishing.

OECD (2005), *OECD Recommendations Concerning Guidelines on Earthquake Safety in Schools*, OECD Publishing.

OECD (2006), *Where Immigrant Students Succeed: A Comparative Review of Performance and Engagement in PISA 2003*, OECD Publishing.

OECD (2006), *Demand-sensitive Schooling? Evidence and Issues,* OECD Publishing.

OECD (2007), *No More Failures: Ten Steps to Equity in Education* (by Simon Field, Malgorzata Kuczera and Beatriz Pont), OECD Publishing.

OECD (2008), *Improving School Leadership: Volume 1: Policy and Practice* (by Beatriz Pont, Deborah Nusche and Hunter Moorman), OECD Publishing.

OECD (2009), *Creating Effective Teaching and Learning Environments: First Results from TALIS*, OECD Publishing.

OECD (2009), *Green at Fifteen? How 15-Year-Olds Perform in Environmental Science and Geoscience in PISA 2006*, OECD Publishing.

OECD (2010), *Education at a Glance 2010: OECD Indicators*, OECD Publishing.

OECD (2010), *Are the New Millennium Learners Making the Grade? Technology Use and Educational Performance in PISA*, OECD Publishing.

OECD (2010), *Improving School Leadership: Volume 3: The Toolkit* (by Louise Stoll and Julie Temperley), OECD Publishing.

OECD (2010), *The Nature of Learning: Using Research to Inspire Practice* (edited by Hanna Dumont, David Istance and Francisco Benavides), OECD Publishing.

OECD (forthcoming), *Quality Time for Students: Learning In and Out of School*, OECD Publishing.

3

Transitions Beyond Initial Education

The OECD has examined arrangements and policies surrounding the transitions beyond compulsory schooling. Extended education to at least completion of the upper secondary cycle is increasingly the norm right now across the OECD countries. Alongside shared patterns are marked differences on such matters as the relative proportions who engage in general or vocational study, as well as the possibilities to combine education with employment. Vocational education and training – which have tended to be neglected in countries compared with general school and university programmes, and which often do not well meet labour market needs – have been the focus for recent OECD review, with a new publication, Learning for Jobs. *OECD policy orientations have stressed the need to improve the existence, diversity, relevance and transparency of different pathways, and the need to integrate them into a lifelong learning perspective, while protecting those left most vulnerable as others advance to further education and employment.*

INTRODUCTION

OECD analyses have shed extensive light on the issues, arrangements and policies surrounding the transitions beyond compulsory schooling. Extended education with at least completion of the upper secondary cycle is increasingly the norm right across the OECD countries. Alongside shared patterns are marked differences on such matters as the relative proportions who engage in general or vocational study, as well as the possibilities to combine education with employment. OECD studies on guidance, information systems and qualifications have shown that there is much scope for improving transitions. Policy orientations have stressed the need to improve the existence, diversity, relevance and transparency of different pathways, while protecting those left most vulnerable as others advance to further education and employment.

Vocational education and training (VET) had not been studied by the OECD so extensively until recently and this has now been addressed with reviews of VET policies and of systemic innovation in the VET field. Work at the secondary level and apprenticeships, encapsulated in the new major report *Learning for Jobs*, will now be extended towards the role of post-secondary and tertiary vocational education in paving pathways to jobs. In the future, the OECD *Skills Strategy* will develop intelligence about national supply chains from the acquisition and development of skills, through their utilisation in labour markets and society more broadly, up to how they feed into better jobs, higher productivity, and ultimately better economic and social outcomes.

KEY FINDINGS

Secondary education has become the dominant experience for 17-year-olds in OECD countries: At age 17, over 8 in 10 young people in OECD countries are in secondary education (83%). In some it is the quasi-totality of the age group at 90% or more (Belgium, the Czech Republic, Finland, Germany, Hungary, Japan, Norway, Poland, the Slovak Republic, Slovenia, Sweden and the partner country Estonia). Seventeen-year-olds in education are only the minority in Mexico (49%) and Turkey (39%). Not all countries have figures for 17-year-olds already in post-secondary non-tertiary education, but among those that do, Austria stands out as having a sizeable minority of this teenage group (12%) transferred to such programmes. And in some countries, a small number have already launched on tertiary education even at this young age (the highest proportions being in Australia [5%], Canada [8%], Greece [9%], Ireland [5%], the Netherlands [6%], New Zealand [4%] and Turkey [6%], but with the partner country the Russian Federation well out ahead at 53%).

📖 *Education at a Glance 2010: OECD Indicators*, 2010, Indicator C1

Very high proportions of young adults – recently in the education system – have now completed upper secondary education, though there are countries where these are still the minority: An average of 80% of 25-34 year-olds in OECD countries now complete at least the upper secondary stage of education (2008). This stands as high as 90% or more in Canada, the Czech Republic, Finland, Korea, Poland, the Slovak Republic, Slovenia, Sweden and Switzerland, as well as in the partner country the Russian Federation. The main watershed of participation in formal education used to be marked by completion of lower secondary schooling but this is clearly now shifting upwards to the next level. This brings the "down-side" of the more acute relative disadvantage for the minority of young people who now leave without finishing upper secondary education. Still only half or fewer of young adults had reached this level of attainment in Mexico (40%), Portugal (47%) and Turkey (40%), and partner country Brazil (50%).

📖 *Education at a Glance 2010: OECD Indicators*, 2010, Indicator A1

Nearly three-quarters of 18-year-olds are still in education across OECD countries (73%), with already over a fifth in post-secondary education: In certain countries, the large majority of the age group continues in secondary education at 18 years of age: 80-90% in the Czech Republic, Denmark, Germany, Norway, Poland and Slovenia, and over 90% in Finland (93%) and Sweden (92%). In others, significant numbers have already embarked on tertiary programmes – a third or more of the age band in Belgium (36%), Canada (36%), Greece (46%), Ireland (34%), the United States (42%) and in partner country the Russian Federation (54%), rising to two-thirds in Korea (67%). Over one-in-five 18-year-olds in Austria (22%) and Ireland (23%) are in non-tertiary post-secondary programmes, compared with the OECD average of 3%.

📖 *Education at a Glance 2010: OECD Indicators*, 2010, Indicator C1

Completion of upper secondary education has become the norm over the past 20-30 years: While the completion of upper secondary education for younger adults stands at about 80% across OECD countries, it was only just over two-thirds for the older 45-54 year-olds in 2008 (68%) and lower still for the 55-64 year-olds at 58%. In certain countries, the increase in attainment between the younger and older adult cohorts separated by 30 years of age is dramatic: in Greece, it goes from 39% to 75%; in Ireland, from 45% to 85%; in Spain, from 29% to 65%. The growth is especially dramatic in Chile, rising from 39% for the older adult group to more than double at 85% for younger adults, and in Korea with 40% for the older adults to a universal 98%.

📖 *Education at a Glance 2010: OECD Indicators*, 2010, Indicator A1

For young adults across OECD countries, very nearly 7 years can now be expected to be spent in education between the ages of 15 and 29: Synthesising current enrolment patterns for young people in their latter teens and twenties, not far off half (6.8 years) of the 15 years between mid-teenage years and the end of their twenties will now be spent in education. Eight years or more of this age span is spent in education in Denmark, Finland, Germany (men), Iceland, the Netherlands, Poland (women), Slovenia, Sweden (women) and the partner country Estonia (women). The "educational expectancy" of this transition age group tends to be longer among young women than young men though there are exceptions to this (Australia, Germany, Japan, Mexico, the Netherlands, New Zealand, Switzerland, Turkey). In Italy, Norway, Slovenia, Sweden and the partner country Estonia, a young woman can expect on average to spend longer in education than a young man by close to a year or more.

📖 *Education at a Glance 2010: OECD Indicators*, 2010, Indicator C3

A relatively even balance between students enrolled in upper secondary general and vocational programmes across OECD countries as a whole hides very large differences across countries: Just over half of upper secondary level students (54.9%) are in "general" and the others are in pre-vocational and vocational tracks. Over 65% are in "general" tracks in Canada, Chile, Greece, Hungary, Iceland, Ireland, Israel, Japan, Korea, Mexico, Portugal and the United Kingdom, and in the partner countries Brazil, Estonia and India. On the other hand, over 65% are in the vocational tracks in Austria, Belgium, the Czech Republic, Finland, the Netherlands and the Slovak Republic.

📖 *Education at a Glance 2010: OECD Indicators*, 2010, Indicator C1

In general, vocational education and training (VET) has been neglected: VET can play a central role in preparing young people for work, developing the skills of adults and responding to the labour-market needs of the economy. Despite this, VET has tended to be marginalised in policy discussions, often overshadowed by the increasing emphasis on general academic education and the role of schools in preparing students for university education. It is also often regarded as of low status by students and the general public. There are very limited data on VET available, especially data that can reliably be compared across countries.

📖 *Learning for Jobs*, 2010, Summary and Policy Messages and Chapter 1

While strong vocational programmes increase competitiveness, many programmes fail to meet labour market needs: Many of the unskilled jobs which existed in OECD countries a generation ago are fast disappearing and OECD countries need to compete on the quality of goods and services they provide. This calls for a labour force well-equipped with middle-level trade, technical and professional skills usually delivered through vocational programmes alongside the high skills associated with university education. But VET systems face major challenges and vocational programmes for young people, often rooted in education institutions, tend to develop their own dynamic and can become too easily separated from the fast-changing world of modern economies.

📖 *Learning for Jobs*, 2010, Summary and Policy Messages and Chapter 2

Figure 3.1.

Completion of upper secondary education is now the norm across OECD countries (2008)

Population that has attained at least upper secondary education, percentage, by age group

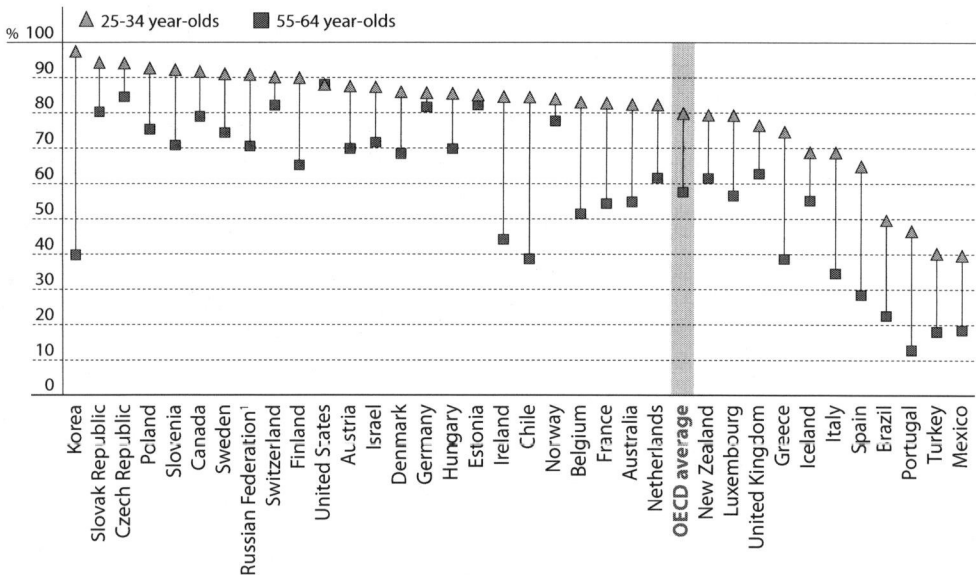

1. Year of reference 2002.
Source: OECD (2010), *Education at a Glance 2010: OECD Indicators*, OECD Publishing.

StatLink 🔗 http://dx.doi.org/10.1787/888932310092

Certain countries do not mix education with employment together for young adults: How the average 6.8 of the 15 years between 15 and 29 years will be experienced – in particular whether it will include being in employment status while also in education – varies sharply from country to country. There are some where these years will be primarily devoted to education without mixing this with employment status. For instance, less than 12 months on average for men and women combined from age 15 to 29 are counted as being in both education and employment in the following countries: Belgium (0.6 in the total 6.9 years in education between these ages), Greece (0.4 in 6.6), Hungary (0.4 in 7.1), Italy (0.6 in 6.8), Japan (0.9 in 5.9 up to the age of 24 years), Luxembourg (0.4 in 7.8), Portugal (0.6 in 6.0), Spain (0.8 in 5.5) and Turkey (0.6 in 3.7).

📖 *Education at a Glance 2010: OECD Indicators*, 2010, Indicator C3

Box 3.1. **Youth and economic crisis**

The economic crisis has affected labour markets in a number of ways. Part-time work has increased, average actual hours worked by the full-time employed have decreased and the number of employees with temporary contracts has decreased in European countries. While the overall unemployment rate among the OECD countries increased by 2.0 percentage points between 2008 and 2009 (from 5.0% to 7.0%), the extent of the increase varies with age and level of education.

The youth population has been the most affected. The unemployment rate for 15-29 year-olds in OECD countries increased on average by 3.3 percentage points, from 10.2% to 13.5%. As a result of the economic crisis, the labour market is becoming more selective and the lack of relevant skills/ experience brings a higher risk of unemployment for recent entrants. The extent of risk varies with the level of education.

Among OECD countries (excluding Chile, Japan, Korea, Mexico and the United States), the lowest increase in the unemployment rate between 2008 and 2009 has been among those with higher levels of education. It increased by 4.8 percentage points for those who did not complete upper secondary education, and by 1.7 percentage points for those who completed tertiary education. Workers with the lowest educational attainment are more likely to be in sectors such as construction or the automobile industry which have been severely affected by the crisis.

Change in unemployment rate for the 15-29 year-old population (2008-09)

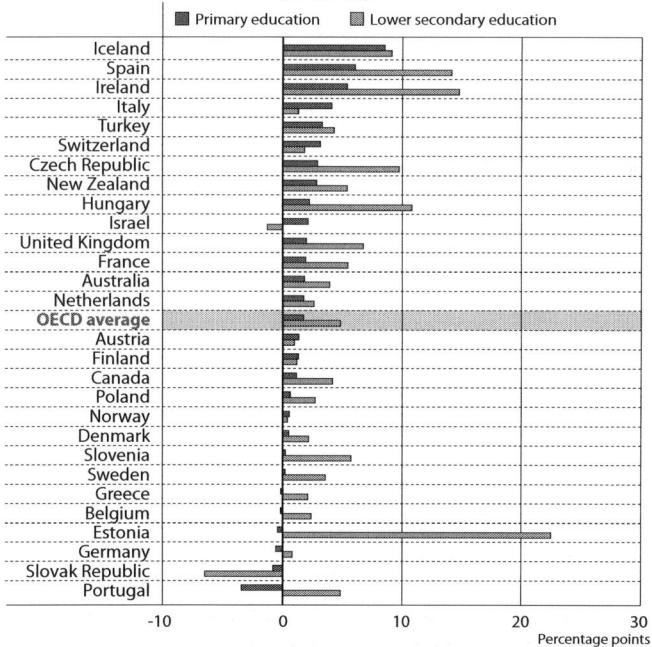

Source: OECD (2010), *Education at a Glance 2010: OECD Indicators*, OECD Publishing; Hijman, R. (2009), "The Impact of the Crisis on Employment", *Statistics in Focus* 79/2009, Eurostat; and OECD (2010), *OECD Employment Outlook 2010*, OECD Publishing.

StatLink ᘔᗏᔕᘯ http://dx.doi.org/10.1787/888932310453

In other countries, being in "education" means being in employment as well for many young people: There are other countries with a "mixed model" where an important part of the years in education are simultaneously in employment, including on work study programmes. In some countries indeed, more than half of this time in education will have the double status combining it with employment (Australia, Denmark, Iceland, the Netherlands and Switzerland).

📖 *Education at a Glance 2010: OECD Indicators*, 2010, Indicator C3

Across the OECD, 7.0% of 15-19 year-olds are not in education or employment, with more than double this level (14.7%) for 20-24 year-olds and significantly more in some countries: The countries where the shares of the teenage group out of education and not employed in 2008 reach double figures are Israel (22.2%), Spain (10.5%) and a high 32.6% in Turkey, with a relatively high level in partner country Brazil (13.8%). The numbers out of education and not employed among adults in their early twenties tend to be significantly higher: near or more than 20% of the 20-24 year-olds are in this situation in Italy (22.0%), Spain (19.4%), with very high levels in Israel (37.5%) and Turkey (44.6%), as well as in partner country Brazil (22.5%).

📖 *Education at a Glance 2010: OECD Indicators*, 2010, Indicator C3

In rapidly-changing economies, career guidance has become more critical but it suffers serious weaknesses in many OECD countries: Young people face a sequence of complex choices over a lifetime of learning and work; helping them to make these decisions is the task of career guidance. But in many countries, career guidance suffers from serious weaknesses. Too often those offering guidance are inadequately acquainted with labour market issues; guidance services can be fragmented, under-resourced and reactive, so that those who most need guidance risk failing to obtain it; many guidance personnel are based in education institutions and may give partial, pro-academic advice; relevant labour market information is too often not available or not readily comprehensible; and the evidence base on "what works" in career guidance is generally weak.

📖 *Learning for Jobs*, 2010, Summary and Policy Messages and Chapter 3

In most countries, there is a drop at upper secondary level in the students with special needs and receiving additional resources, compared with the primary and lower secondary levels: For students with disabilities, a median of 1.6% receive additional funding at this level as against 3.3% for lower secondary. (The only exception to the drop between levels among the countries with data is England.) Similarly, the proportion getting additional financial resources specifically for learning difficulties is lower at the upper than the lower secondary level, again with the exception of England. For those recognised as having disadvantages and being thereby entitled to additional resources, there is again a drop between the two levels in most countries, with only the Slovak Republic showing a marginal increase from lower to upper secondary.

📖 *Students with Disabilities, Learning Difficulties and Disadvantages: Policies, Statistics and Indicators – 2007 Edition*, 2008, Chapter 4

There is an important gap between the developed cognitive capacity in mid-teenagers ("high horsepower") and their emotional maturity ("poor steering"): The insights provided by neuroscience on adolescence are especially important as this is the period when so much takes place in an individual's educational career. The secondary phase of education brings key decisions to be made with long-lasting consequences regarding personal, educational and career options. At this time, young people are already well-developed in terms of cognitive capacity ("high horsepower") but they are immature ("poor steering"), not just because of inexperience, but because of under-developed neurological emotional development.

📖 *Understanding the Brain: The Birth of a Learning Science*, 2007, Conclusions and Future Prospects

POLICY DIRECTIONS

The lifelong learning approach entails a broad conception of foundation learning at the end of the secondary cycle: Most countries report reforms in this area that are aimed at raising the level of qualification of school-leavers and retaining more young people in upper secondary education. These include:

- **Increasing the relevance of initial education to work and the value of work-related qualifications in the job market:** This general aim to create a better match between the objectives of education systems and the needs of the firm can be done in various ways, including, for instance, the broadening and development of new frameworks for vocational education for young people in schools (as in Australia) or through reinforcing collaboration between the different partners (as in the reform of the dual system in the French Community of Belgium).

- **Broadening criteria for reforming school qualifications:** Looking beyond particular knowledge or competence sets, reforms include: the recognition of prior learning (*e.g.* Australia); the recognition of achievement across a whole programme rather than specific subject attainment (*e.g.* Ireland); and the development of a national certificate using "achievement standards" developed for the school curriculum and unit standards from the national qualifications framework (*e.g.* New Zealand).

- **Developing better progression routes for young people within and between qualifications:** Examples include enabling the easier vertical and horizontal transfer from one educational level to another (Slovenia), and flexible dual trajectories combining learning and work (the Netherlands).

📖 *Qualifications Systems: Bridges to Lifelong Learning*, 2007, Chapter 2

The recent VET study has synthesised wide-ranging analysis and review into five key recommendations. These include:

- **Provide the right mix of skills for the labour market:** Provide a mix of VET training places that reflect both student preferences and employer needs, and share the costs of doing so between government, employers and individuals according to who will benefit. Engage employers and unions in curriculum development to ensure that the skills taught correspond to those needed in the modern workplace while also ensuring that the VET fosters generic, transferable skills and that students in vocational programmes have adequate numeracy and literacy skills.

- **Reform career guidance to deliver well-informed career advice for all:** Develop a coherent career guidance profession, independent from psychological counselling and well-informed by labour market information. Recognise the importance of guidance by resourcing and evaluating it adequately, and ensure objective and abundant information about careers and courses, including through partnerships with employers.

- **Recruit sufficient numbers of teachers and trainers, and ensure they are well-acquainted with modern employment needs and are pedagogically prepared:** Promote flexible pathways of recruitment and facilitate the entry of those with industry skills into the VET teacher workforce. Provide appropriate pedagogical preparation for trainers, adapted to the learning being provided. Encourage part-time working and interchange between VET institutions and industry, so that vocational teachers can update their knowledge, and trainers in firms spend time in VET institutions to enhance their pedagogical skills.

- **Make full use of workplace learning:** Make substantial use of workplace training in initial VET, ensuring that the system encourages participation by both employers and students, and that the training is of good quality, (with effective quality assurance and a clear contractual framework for apprenticeships). Sustain workplace training and respond to increased demand for full-time VET during the difficult economic climate.

- **Support the VET system by engaging stakeholders and promoting transparency:** Systematically engage with employers, trade unions and other key stakeholders in VET policy and provision and qualification frameworks, strengthening quality assurance and adopting national assessment frameworks to underpin consistent quality. Strengthen data on the labour market outcomes of VET, and the institutional capacity to use that data.

📖 *Learning for Jobs,* 2010, Chapters 2-6 and Executive Summary

Recognise the gap between the cognitive capacity and emotional maturity in teenagers to avoid definitive choices: The gap between intellectual and emotional capacity cannot imply that important choices should simply be delayed until adulthood when the gap closes. It does suggest, with the additional powerful weight of neurological evidence, that the options taken should not take the form of definitively closing doors.

📖 *Understanding the Brain: The Birth of a Learning Science,* 2007, Chapter 2

References

Hijman, R. (2009), "The Impact of the Crisis on Employment", *Statistics in Focus* 79/2009, Eurostat.

OECD (2007), *Understanding the Brain: The Birth of a Learning Science*, OECD Publishing.

OECD (2007), *Qualifications Systems: Bridges to Lifelong Learning*, OECD Publishing.

OECD (2008), *Students with Disabilities, Learning Difficulties and Disadvantages: Policies, Statistics and Indicators – 2007 Edition*, OECD Publishing.

OECD (2010), *Education at a Glance 2010: OECD Indicators*, OECD Publishing.

OECD (2010), *OECD Employment Outlook 2010,* OECD Publishing.

OECD (2010), *Learning for Jobs*, OECD Publishing.

4

HIGHER EDUCATION

Countries have shared the very rapid expansion of higher or tertiary education, which means that instead of this being an experience enjoyed by a privileged minority, it has now become even the majority experience of each new cohort. There are broad trends visible across the OECD – for instance, the growing international tertiary education market and the greater formalisation of quality assurance. Despite rising costs for the individual, tertiary education remains a primarily public enterprise in most countries. There has been prominent OECD work on higher education, including on internationalisation, a major review of tertiary education, the regional role of higher education institutions (HEIs), the future of higher education, and feasibility work on the Assessment of Higher Education Learning Outcomes (AHELO). Policy orientations include the need to develop and work towards strategic visions, to ensure that quality assurance serves both improvement and accountability purposes, and to use cost-sharing between the state and students as the principle to shape the sector's funding.

INTRODUCTION

Countries share the very rapid expansion of higher or tertiary education, which means that instead of this being an experience enjoyed by a privileged minority, it has now become even the majority experience of each new cohort. There are other broad trends visible across the OECD – for instance, the growing international tertiary education market and the greater formalisation of quality assurance. A major review of tertiary education was completed in 2008 and published in two volumes. The feasibility study for the international Assessment of Higher Education Learning Outcomes (AHELO) is breaking new ground in assessing learning outcomes internationally. Reviews of higher education in regions and cities' development are showing the benefits of stronger interaction and engagement between institutions and local actors to reinforce social and economic development.

There has been long-running work on internationalisation of higher education at the OECD, including statistical development and analysis, policy evaluation, and the formulation of the OECD/UNESCO *Guidelines for Quality Provision in Cross-border Higher Education*. Work on "University Futures" has identified scenarios for the future, and examined trends on globalisation, demography and technology in higher education.

Policy orientations emerging from this large body of work include the need to develop and work towards strategic visions, to ensure that quality assurance serves both improvement and accountability purposes, and to use cost-sharing between the state and students as the principle to shape the sector's funding.

KEY FINDINGS

Many more young adults are now in education even compared with a decade ago, accounting for a quarter of 20-29 year-olds and with university programme entry up more than 20 percentage points since the mid-1990s: An average of one quarter of young adults aged 20-29 are enrolled in education across OECD countries, and 30% or more are in Australia, Denmark, Finland, Iceland, Poland, Slovenia and Sweden (2008). In contrast, only Denmark had 30% of 20-29 year-olds enrolled in education in 1995. Enrolment among 20-29 year-olds doubled or more since then in the Czech Republic, Greece and Hungary. Entry rates to university-level education went up by nearly 20 percentage points across the OECD since 1995, and by more than 20 points since 2000 in Australia, the Czech Republic, Korea, the Slovak Republic and the United States.

📖 *Education at a Glance 2010: OECD Indicators*, 2010, Indicators A2 and C1

Over half the population of OECD countries will participate in university-level education at some stage of their lives based on current patterns of entry: Participation rates in university education of over 50% for a single age cohort are becoming the benchmark for OECD countries, with 56% for OECD countries overall. (This refers to "net entry rates" which are calculated as the proportion in a synthetic age cohort who go into university-type education at some point in their lives based on current enrolment patterns.) For some countries in 2008, such entry rates are substantially higher again: 70% or over can expect to enter university-type programmes (tertiary-type A) alone in Australia, Finland, Iceland, Korea, New Zealand, Norway, Poland, Portugal and the Slovak Republic.

📖 *Education at a Glance 2010: OECD Indicators*, 2010, Indicator A2; *Tertiary Education for the Knowledge Society: Volume 1*, 2008, Chapter 2

Nearly a third of university students fail to graduate and such "dropout" is higher still in non-university tertiary programmes: On average across the 23 OECD countries for which data are available, some 30% of university (tertiary-type A) students fail to successfully complete the programmes they undertake.

Figure 4.1.
Population that has attained tertiary education (2008)
Percentage, by age group

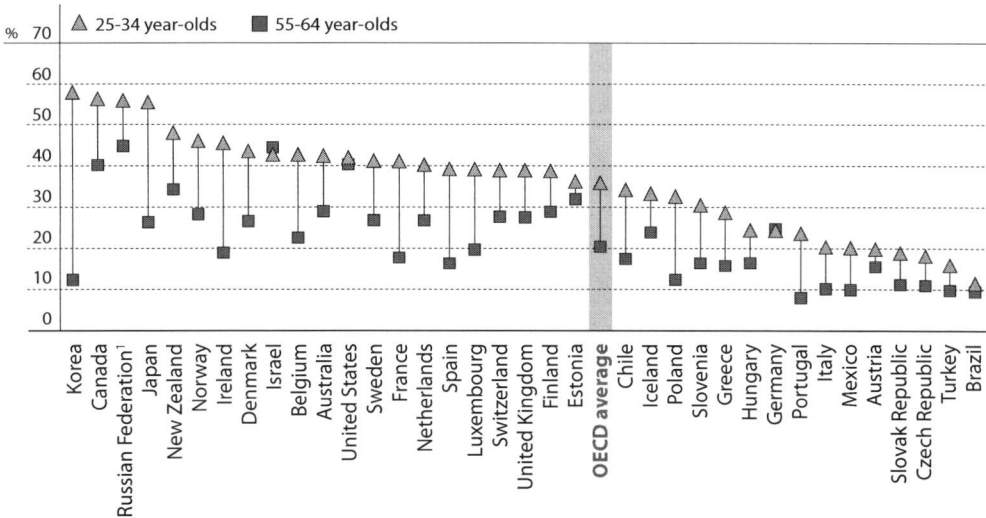

1. Year of reference 2002.

Source: OECD (2010), *Education at a Glance 2010: OECD Indicators*, OECD Publishing.

StatLink ⬛᠍᠍⬛ http://dx.doi.org/10.1787/888932310092

Completion rates differ widely. The countries where over three-quarters of university students complete the programme are Japan (93%), followed by Portugal (86%), Korea (84%), Denmark (82%), the United Kingdom (81%), Australia (80%), Spain (79%) and partner country the Russian Federation (80%). In contrast, in Mexico, New Zealand, Sweden and the United States less that six in ten of those who enter go on to complete (though for Sweden it includes those enrolled in single courses who do not intend to do the full programme). The non-completion rate in vocational, non-university programmes stands even higher than in university-type programmes at 38%, and is highest in New Zealand and the United States at around two-thirds, and in Portugal at over 80%.

📖 *Education at a Glance 2010: OECD Indicators*, 2010, Indicator A4

Nearly one third of expenditure on educational institutions across the OECD is for tertiary education, accounting in some for 2% or more of their GDP: Large differences between countries in the size of systems, pathways available to students, programme durations and the organisation of teaching, mean that there are large differences in the level of expenditure which countries spend on higher education. Canada, Chile, Korea and the United States spend the most on higher education institutions, at 2.0% or more of their GDP. In three of these cases, the majority share comes from private sources: in Chile (1.7% of GDP), Korea (1.9%) and the United States (2.1%).

📖 *Education at a Glance 2010: OECD Indicators*, 2010, Indicator B2

Tertiary education is still predominantly a public enterprise in the OECD area: There has been no general decline in enrolments, funding or public funding in public tertiary education in OECD countries. Except for Japan and Korea, tertiary education is still predominantly a public enterprise: the private for-profit sector is still marginal in the large majority of countries, and even more so for advanced research programmes. At the time of writing, tertiary education institutions had not faced a major decline in public funding either; instead, their budgets have increased over recent years, in most cases per student as well as in total. Students and their households have nevertheless felt serious changes as they contribute more to the expenditures of tertiary education institutions than they used to. In most countries, however, tertiary education is still significantly publicly subsidised.

📖 *Higher Education to 2030 – Volume 2, Globalisation*, 2009, Chapter 9

OECD analysis has identified five groups of countries in their approach to assisting students financially: Of the countries participating in the OECD Tertiary Education Review, first there are those which base their student support exclusively on a public loan fund without grants (Iceland and Norway). A second group – Australia, Japan, the Netherlands, New Zealand, Sweden and the United Kingdom – combine a public loan system with a publicly-funded grant scheme. A third group – Finland, Poland, Portugal and the partner country Estonia – is like the second except that the loans are provided by commercial banks with public subsidy and/or public guarantee. A fourth group of countries – Chile, China and Korea – offer a wide choice of schemes through a mix of a public loan fund, commercial banks and grants. A fifth group – the Flemish Community of Belgium, Croatia, the Czech Republic, Greece, Mexico, the Russian Federation, Spain and Switzerland – has no loan scheme and base student support on grants.

📖 *Tertiary Education for the Knowledge Society: Volume 1*, 2008, Chapter 4

There has been more than a fourfold increase in foreign students since the mid-1970s, highly concentrated in a small number of destination countries and making up 15% or more of tertiary students in several: In the 1990s, there was a sharp increase in the international mobility of students and teachers, educational programmes and higher education institutions which has continued since. The number of foreign students worldwide stood at around 0.8 million in 1975 and has now risen to an estimated 3.3 million by 2008. Foreign students are highly concentrated in a few countries. Half attend higher education in the top five destination countries (United States, United Kingdom, Germany, France and Australia), with another 14% accounted for by the next three (Canada [6%], Japan [4%] and partner country the Russian Federation [4%]). Foreign students make up around 15% or more of the tertiary student body in Australia (20.6%), Austria (15.5%), Switzerland (14.1%) and the United Kingdom (14.7%). In absolute terms, the largest numbers of international students are from China and India.

📖 *Education at a Glance 2010: OECD Indicators*, 2010, Indicator C2

Despite the major demographic changes taking place in OECD countries, the evolution of the academic workforce is not primarily a reflection of these wider demographic trends: The age pyramid of academic staff reflects less the ageing of populations in general and more of an employment system in higher education whose hallmark is permanence with efforts to maintain relatively fixed student-teacher ratios. Similarly, the changing composition of academic staff reflects less general demographic developments and more the diversification of the profession, and the restructuring of relationships between academics and their institutions.

📖 *Higher Education to 2030, Volume 1, Demography*, 2008, Chapters 3 and 4

Figure 4.2.

Distribution of foreign students in tertiary education, by country of destination (2008)

Percentage of foreign tertiary students reported to the OECD who are enrolled in each country of destination

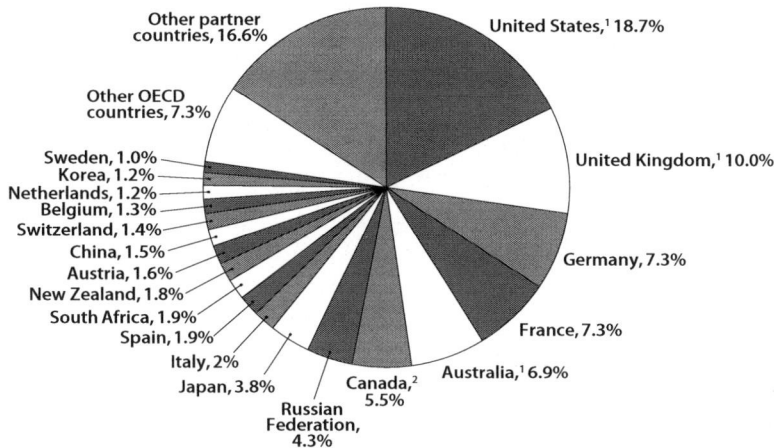

Other partner countries, 16.6%
United States,[1] 18.7%
Other OECD countries, 7.3%
Sweden, 1.0%
Korea, 1.2%
Netherlands, 1.2%
Belgium, 1.3%
Switzerland, 1.4%
China, 1.5%
Austria, 1.6%
New Zealand, 1.8%
South Africa, 1.9%
Spain, 1.9%
Italy, 2%
Japan, 3.8%
Russian Federation, 4.3%
Canada,[2] 5.5%
Australia,[1] 6.9%
France, 7.3%
Germany, 7.3%
United Kingdom,[1] 10.0%

1. Data relate to international students defined on the basis of their country of residence.
2. Year of reference 2007.

Source: OECD (2010), *Education at a Glance 2010: OECD Indicators*, OECD Publishing.

StatLink ﷯ http://dx.doi.org/10.1787/888932310434

Quality assurance in higher education is becoming universalised: The increase in the growth of the number of external quality agencies over the period can be observed through membership of the International Network of Quality Assurance Agencies in Higher Education (INQAAHE). Its core members are the regional and national quality assurance and accreditation agencies, plus associate members of organisations with a strong interest in quality assurance in higher education. This Network was established in 1991, originally with members from only 11 countries, representing most of those with systems, full or partial, of external quality assurance in higher education. By mid-2008 the Network had grown to 154 members from 78 countries, and there are yet other agencies that have not joined the network and some other countries still in the course of developing their systems of quality assurance.

📖 *Higher Education to 2030, Volume 2, Globalisation*, 2009, Chapter 11; Hazelkorn and Marginson in *Higher Education and Policy: Journal of the [OECD] Programme on Institutional Management in Higher Education*, 2009

POLICY DIRECTIONS

While recognising differences of culture and approach in national tertiary education systems, there is a number of common main elements that underpin sound planning and policy making:

- **Develop and articulate a vision for tertiary education:** Countries should as a priority develop a comprehensive and coherent vision for the future of tertiary education, to guide the medium- and long-term in harmony with national social and economic objectives. Ideally, it should result from a systematic review and entail a clear statement of strategic aims.

- **Establish sound instruments for steering towards and implementing that vision:** Tertiary education authorities need to develop their review and monitoring capacity for the system as a whole as opposed to the standard instruments of institutional administration. Within the overall vision, steering instruments need to establish a balance between institutional autonomy and public accountability. Allowing the play of student choice can improve quality and efficiency.
- **Strengthen the ability of institutions to align with the national tertiary education strategy:** Institutions should be encouraged to develop an outward focus, including via external representation on their governing bodies, and be required to establish strategic plans. The national policy framework should give institutions the means to manage effectively their wider responsibilities.

📖 *Tertiary Education for the Knowledge Society: Volume 1*, 2008, Chapter 3

Lessons drawn from OECD review about the implementation of tertiary education reforms suggest that it should:
- **Recognise the different viewpoints of stakeholders** through iterative policy development.
- **Allow for bottom-up initiatives** to come forward as proposals by independent committees.
- **Establish ad-hoc independent committees** to initiate tertiary education reforms and involve stakeholders.
- **Use pilots and experimentation.**
- **Favour incremental reforms** over comprehensive overhauls unless there is wide public support for change.
- **Avoid reforms with concentrated costs and diffused benefits.**
- **Identify potential losers** from tertiary education reform and build in compensatory mechanisms.
- **Create conditions for and support the successful implementation of reforms.**
- **Ensure communication about the benefits of reform and the costs of inaction.**
- **Implement the full package of policy proposals.**

📖 *Tertiary Education for the Knowledge Society: Volume 2*, 2008, Chapter 11

Among the principles and pointers for quality assurance in tertiary education, in addition to the general requisites of building the focus on student outcomes and the capacity for quality assurance, are:
- **Ensure that quality assurance serves both improvement and accountability purposes,** and more generally make sure it is consistent with the goals of tertiary education.
- **Combine internal and external mechanisms** for quality assurance.
- **Make stakeholders visible in the evaluation procedures** – students, graduates and employers.
- **Enhance the international comparability** of the quality assurance framework.

📖 *Tertiary Education for the Knowledge Society: Volume 1*, 2008, Chapter 5

Effective initiatives to improve teaching quality in higher education depend above all on the commitment of leaders and management in the institution: Initiatives aimed explicitly at addressing the quality of teaching in higher education fall under three main headings: *i)* institution-wide and quality assurance policies; *ii)* programme monitoring; and *iii)* teaching and learning support. An institution aiming to pursue a teaching quality strategy will often set up a specific organisation, supported by technical staff for the design of appropriate instruments, as a first step. The success of such initiatives depends mainly, however, on the commitment of heads of departments.

📖 *Learning our Lesson: Review of Quality Teaching in Higher Education*, 2010, Executive Summary

Among the main principles guiding funding strategies in tertiary education, beyond ensuring that they promote the wider goals and societal benefit, are:

- **Use cost-sharing between the state and students as the principle to shape the sector's funding:** There is need for public subsidies to tertiary education regardless of the sector of provision, but also for charging tuition fees to students, especially if limited public funds would ration student numbers, jeopardise spending levels per student, or restrict financial support for the disadvantaged.

- **Make institutional funding to teaching formula-driven:** The criteria for the distribution of funds to institutions need to be clear, using transparent formulae which shield allocation decisions from political pressures, while tailoring incentives to shape institutional plans towards national goals.

- **Improve cost-effectiveness:** Inefficiencies should be addressed through such means as: linking funding more closely to graduation rates, reducing public subsidies for those who stay too long in their studies; eliminating some duplicated programmes; rationalising low- or declining-enrolment programmes; increasing the use of shared facilities; and expanding student mobility across institutions.

- **Back the overall funding approach with a comprehensive student support system:** A mixed system of grants and loans assists students in covering tuition and living costs, alleviating excessive hours in paid work or disproportionate reliance on family support. In many countries student support needs to be expanded and diversified.

📖 *Tertiary Education for the Knowledge Society: Volume 1*, 2008, Chapter 4

An internationalisation policy centred on importing higher education is more appropriate for many countries which cannot afford to base policies on exporting higher education: The benefits to a country of a developed international policy are especially obvious in those countries which are net "exporters". Some countries may adopt the "skilled migration" approach of attracting talented students and academics to promote the knowledge economy, and the "revenue-generating" approach aimed at growing the opportunities for advanced human capital investment using income from foreign students' fees. The "capacity-building" approach, on the other hand, encourages the use of imported higher education as a relatively quick way to build an emerging country's capacity and this has proved particularly effective in several Asian and Middle Eastern countries.

📖 *Education Policy Analysis 2006: Focus on Higher Education*, 2006, Chapter 2

In the international market for higher education, the different stakeholders each need to contribute to protect students from low-quality provision and disreputable providers: The OECD in close co-operation with UNESCO published a set of international *Guidelines for Quality Provision in Cross-border Higher Education* in 2005 recommending actions for different stakeholders. For governments, it is recommended that they:

- **Establish or encourage the establishment of a comprehensive, fair and transparent system of registration or licensing** for cross-border higher education providers wishing to operate in their territory.

- **Establish or encourage the establishment of a comprehensive capacity for reliable quality assurance and accreditation** of cross-border higher education provision.

- **Consult and co-ordinate amongst the various competent bodies for quality assurance and accreditation,** both nationally and internationally.

- **Provide accurate, reliable and easily accessible information on the criteria and standards for registration, licensure, quality assurance and accreditation** of cross-border higher education, their consequences on the funding of students, institutions or programmes where applicable, and their voluntary or mandatory nature.

- Consider becoming party to, and contribute to, **the development and/or updating of the appropriate UNESCO regional conventions on recognition of qualifications,** and establish national information centres as stipulated by the conventions.

- Where appropriate **develop or encourage bilateral or multilateral recognition agreements,** facilitating the recognition or equivalence of each country's qualifications based on the procedures and criteria included in mutual agreements.

- Contribute to efforts to improve the **accessibility at the international level of up-to-date, accurate and comprehensive information on recognised higher education institutions/providers.**

Recognising partial outcomes and non-formal and informal learning represent ways for tertiary education to improve efficiency and equity: A considerable number of students prematurely abandon their studies or do not complete the courses they began. Recognition of accumulated learning outcomes is one way of rationalising post-secondary education and making it less expensive. Many countries or regions use the recognition of non-formal and informal learning outcomes to grant course exemptions for those returning to tertiary education which may be extended to those who changed their course prior to its completion. Recognition of non-formal and informal learning outcomes can broaden the group of potential entrants and help to offset the decrease in enrolments among traditional students arriving from schooling.

📖 *Recognising Non-Formal and Informal Learning: Outcomes, Policies and Practices,* 2010, Chapter 3

Government has a key role to play in joining up a wide range of policies and in creating supportive environments to promote the regional role of higher education institutions. These include to:

- **Create more "joined up" decision making** (finance, education, science and technology, and industry ministries, etc.) to co-ordinate decisions on priorities and strategies in regional development.

- **Make regional engagement and its agenda for economic, social and cultural development explicit** in higher education legislation and mission strategies.

- **Develop indicators and monitor outcomes** to assess the impact of higher education institutions on regional performance, and encourage their participation in regional governance structures.

- **Provide a supportive regulatory, tax and accountability environment** for university-enterprise co-operation.

Higher education institutions themselves should change so that what is now active regional engagement in particularly forward-looking and entrepreneurial institutions becomes more widespread across the sector.

📖 *Higher Education and Regions: Globally Competitive, Locally Engaged,* 2007, Chapter 9

References

Hazelkorn, E. (2009), "Rankings and the Battle for World-Class Excellence: Institutional Strategies and Policy Choices", *Higher Education and Policy: Journal of the Programme on Institutional Management in Higher Education*, Vol. 21, No. 1, OECD Publishing.

Marginson, S. (2009), "The Knowledge Economy and Higher Education: A System for Regulating the Value of Knowledge", *Higher Education and Policy: Journal of the Programme on Institutional Management in Higher Education*, Vol. 21, No. 1, OECD Publishing.

OECD/UNESCO (2005), *Guidelines for Quality Provision in Cross-border Higher Education.*

OECD (2006), *Education Policy Analysis 2006: Focus on Higher Education*, OECD Publishing.

OECD (2007), *Higher Education and Regions: Globally Competitive, Locally Engaged*, OECD Publishing.

OECD (2008), *Tertiary Education for the Knowledge Society* (by Paulo Santiago, Karine Tremblay, Ester Basri and Elena Amal), OECD Publishing.

OECD (2008), *Higher Education to 2030, Volume 1, Demography*, OECD Publishing.

OECD (2009), *Higher Education to 2030, Volume 2, Globalisation*, OECD Publishing.

OECD (2010), *Recognising Non-formal and Informal Learning: Outcomes, Polices and Practices* (edited by Patrick Werquin), OECD Publishing.

OECD (2010), *Learning our Lesson: Review of Quality Teaching in Higher Education* (by Fabrice Hénard), OECD Publishing.

OECD (2010), *Education at a Glance 2010: OECD Indicators*, OECD Publishing.

5

Lifelong Learning and Adults

This chapter draws on various sources to examine evidence and recommendations regarding adult education and training, and lifelong learning more widely. It brings together survey information on individuals in the adult population, education system information, enterprise data, and research findings on the ageing process. Wide differences exist between countries in which organised learning is a common adult activity and where it remains much less common. The majority of the learning undertaken relates to non-formal job-related training, and in the formal education sector there are countries where very few older adults are found. Studies of ageing show the clear benefits of continued learning. Findings and conclusions from OECD studies on key areas such as financing (especially co-financing), guidance, the recognition of non-formal learning, and qualifications systems are presented, some of these from the mid-2000s.

INTRODUCTION

With agreement on the importance of lifelong learning in the OECD and by countries, it is natural that adult participation in education and training has been a focus of statistical work, research and policy analysis. The international data show how wide the variations between countries are in terms of adult participation in formal and non-formal education, with very marked differences according to the qualification levels of the adults, and also by age (see also Chapter 7). Lifelong learning has been a defining goal for education and training policies for many years, emphasising the need for organised learning to take place over the whole lifespan and across the different main spheres that make up our lives ("life-wide"). Despite acknowledgement of its importance, holistic analyses of lifelong learning have been less a feature of OECD work in recent years.

The OECD has conducted international reviews bringing together the education and employment perspectives on provision and policies for adult learning, with complementary studies on qualifications, financing and the recognition of non-formal and informal learning. The ambitious Programme for the International Assessment of Adult Competencies (PIAAC) is underway and aims to publish a powerful comparative data set on human capital in 2013. With information from 5 000 participants in each country, PIAAC will cover: key cognitive skills; educational attainment and skill formation; skill use in the workplace and elsewhere; labour market outcomes; characteristics of individuals; and changes in literacy and numeracy skills over time.

KEY FINDINGS

Only a minority of adults engage in organised formal or non-formal learning over the course of a year: Combining formal and non-formal education and training, only a minority of adults participated in such learning activity over a year across OECD countries as a whole (41% in 2007), even when "education" is widely understood to include short seminars, lectures or workshops. In only seven countries do around half or more of adults engage in organised learning (Finland, New Zealand, Norway, Sweden, Switzerland, the United Kingdom and the United States). The gap is very wide between the OECD country with the highest engagement in adult learning (Sweden at 73%) and Hungary with only 9%. As these are overall averages, they hide still wider variations between adults of different ages or levels of educational attainment.

📖 *Education at a Glance 2010: OECD Indicators*, 2010, Indicator A5

Only 1 in 15 adults aged 30-39 is enrolled either full- or part-time in formal education in OECD countries, and students make up no more than 1.6% of the 40+ age group: The 20-29 year-olds enrolled in education, while all are "adults", include many who are completing their initial cycles of education and training. For older adults, 5.9% of the 30-39 year-olds across OECD countries are enrolled in education, full- or part-time. It is significantly higher than this in certain countries at more than 1 in 10: Australia (13.4%), Finland (15.0%), Iceland (12.8%), New Zealand (11.9%) and Sweden (12.5%). Some countries are unable to make the corresponding calculations for the 40+ age group, but where they can, the highest levels of enrolment are found in Australia (5.8%), Belgium (3.9%), Finland (3.5%), Iceland (3.9%) and New Zealand (5.2%).

📖 *Education at a Glance 2010: OECD Indicators*, 2010, Indicator C1

There are countries where to be enrolled in formal education as an older adult remains a very rare occurrence: With an OECD average of just under 6% for adults in their thirties in formal education, there are naturally countries where the level is significantly lower. Those at half or less below the average

enrolment rate for 30-39 year-olds include: France (2.6%), Germany (2.5%), Korea (2.1%), Luxembourg (0.8%), the Netherlands (2.8%) and Turkey (1.8%). Lack of data prevent a number of OECD countries from making the corresponding calculations for the 40+ age group; where they can do so, 0.5% or fewer of these mature adults are in full- or part-time education in the Czech Republic, Germany, Ireland, Italy, Korea, Luxembourg, Switzerland and Turkey.

📖 *Education at a Glance 2010: OECD Indicators*, 2010, Indicator C1

Across the OECD, just over a quarter of working-age adults have recently participated in job-related learning, with the highest levels in some Nordic countries: A comfortable majority of the participants in adult educational activities are found in work-related learning. In 2007, just over a quarter of OECD population aged 25-64 (28%) in OECD countries participated in job-related non-formal education. The country variations are wide. The high countries at over 40% are Finland (44%), Norway (47%) and Sweden (61%), with Germany and the Slovak Republic not far behind at 38%. Less than 15% of adults participated in job-related learning in Greece (11%), Hungary (6%), Italy (14%) and Korea (11%), with Poland and Portugal also under 20%. As to be expected, participation in such forms of learning is significantly higher among those in employment (36%) than the unemployed (16%) across OECD countries as a whole, and somewhat higher among men (30%) than women (27%).

📖 *Education at a Glance 2010: OECD Indicators*, 2010, Indicator A5

Figure 5.1.

Participation in formal and/or non-formal education, by adults aged 25-64 years-old and educational attainment (2007)

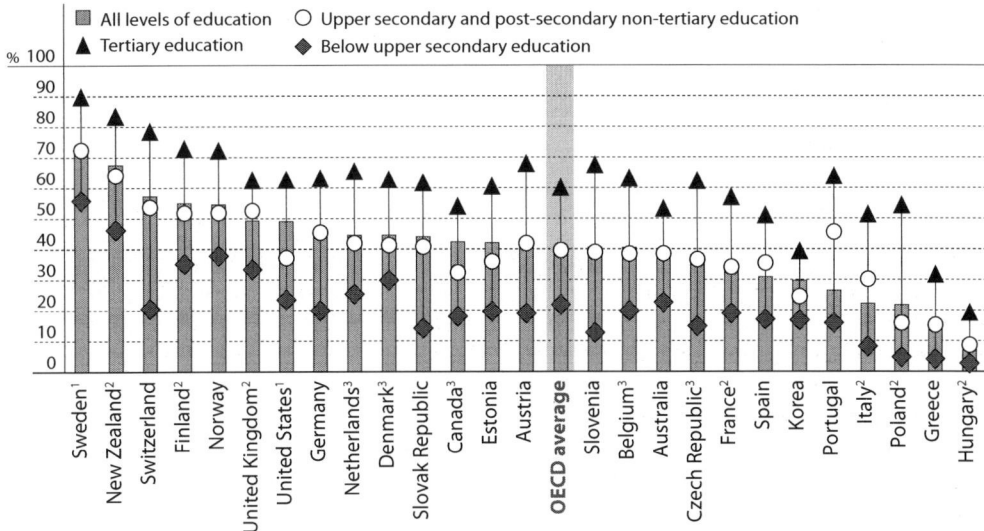

1. Year of reference 2005.
2. Year of reference 2006.
3. Year of reference 2008.
Source: OECD (2010), *Education at a Glance 2010: OECD Indicators*, OECD Publishing.

StatLink ⬛⬛ http://dx.doi.org/10.1787/888932310168

Despite the common emphasis on constructing knowledge-based economies, there has been a slight downward trend in Europe in jobs using high levels of learning, discretion and complexity: European Survey of Working Conditions data show that while a large share of European workers have access to work settings that call for learning and problem solving, there has been a slight downward trend over the decade from 1995 in the proportion of employees having access to work settings characterised by high levels of learning, complexity and discretion. There are important variations in the spread of learning organisations across the European Union, ranging from 65% of salaried employees in such organisations in Sweden in 2005 to only around 20% in Spain among OECD countries.

📖 *Innovative Workplaces: Learning Organisations and Innovation*, forthcoming, Chapter 6

Insufficient opportunities for education are not the principal reason why many adults do not engage in learning: Evidence on barriers to participation suggests that under-investment in adult learning is due more to the demand side than to lack of supply of learning opportunities. Many adults are simply not interested. This can be because they are not aware of the need for training or because of lack of information, lack of incentives or a perceived lack of returns. When asked about the obstacles, most refer to the key problem of lack of time, mainly due to work or family obligations (the opportunity costs). Lack of resources to pay for training is another issue. The time required for training and the resulting opportunity costs could be reduced through more systematic recognition of acquired skills and competences, more efficient forms of training, individualised programmes of study, and more effective information and advice. Co-financing can help to share the time costs for training as well as the direct costs.

📖 *Promoting Adult Learning*, 2005, Chapter 5

Brain research provides important additional support for adults' continued learning throughout the lifespan: One of the most powerful set of neurological findings on learning concerns the brain's remarkable properties of "plasticity" – to grow in response to experience and to prune itself when parts become unnecessary. This continues throughout the lifespan, and far further into old age than had previously been understood. The demands made on the individual and on his/her learning are key to the plasticity – the more one learns, the more one can learn. Neuroscience has shown that learning is a lifelong activity in which the more that it continues, the more effective it is.

📖 *Understanding the Brain: The Birth of a Learning Science*, 2007, Chapter 2

Brain research confirms the wider benefits of learning, especially for ageing populations: For older people, cognitive engagement, regular physical exercise and an active social life promote learning and can delay degeneration of the ageing brain. The enormous and costly problems represented by dementia in ever-ageing populations can be addressed through the learning interventions being identified through neuroscience. Combinations of improved diagnostics, opportunities to exercise, appropriate and validated pharmacological treatment, and good educational intervention can do much to maintain positive well-being and to prevent deterioration.

📖 *Understanding the Brain: The Birth of a Learning Science*, 2007, Chapter 2

POLICY DIRECTIONS

The lifelong learning framework offers directions for policy reform to address five systemic features:

- **Improving access, quality and equity:** Gaps in access are especially clear as regards very young children and older adults at either side of the main initial education system, and these gaps need to be addressed. Access is not simply a matter of enrolment, however, and includes both the quality of the provision involved and the equity to ensure a fair and inclusive distribution of opportunities.

- **Ensuring foundation skills for all:** This requires not just universal access to basic education, but improvements in young people's motivation to learn and their capacity for independent learning. Foundation skills are also needed by those adults who lack them.

- **Recognising all forms of learning, not just formal courses of study:** Learning takes many forms and occurs in many different settings, from formal courses in schools or colleges to various types of experience in families, communities and workplaces. All types of learning need to be recognised and made visible, according to their content, quality and outcomes, rather than their location and form.

- **Mobilising resources, rethinking resource allocation across all sectors, settings and over the life-cycle:** Given that higher levels of participation increase costs, countries have used many different approaches to reduce them, especially teaching and personnel costs, rationalisation of the structure of provision, better use of ICTs, and more extensive use of the private sector.

- **Ensuring collaboration among a wide range of partners:** All lifelong learning involves stakeholders well beyond those covered by the educational authorities, and co-ordination in policy development and implementation is essential for success.

📖 "Lifelong Learning", *Policy Brief*, 2004

Developing and co-ordinating system-level policies for effective adult learning, especially engaging at-risk groups, means:

- **Developing adult learners at young ages:** This means considering as an entire portfolio the range of interventions to combat low adult attainment (training programmes, school-based policies and earlier interventions). It means reducing the rate of dropout at school level and getting those young adults who do drop out of school back into second-chance opportunities as early as possible.

- **Working towards compatibility between training and employment:** In many countries, labour market programmes and the education system are independent, with few links to permit the training involved to count towards conventional qualifications. Linking the two can facilitate the move not just into work, but into more solid careers.

- **Linking adult learning to social welfare programmes:** This is an integral aspect of active programmes – to shift away from passive welfare transfers towards training alternatives which strengthen labour market prospects. The linking of adult learning and welfare benefits policies is part of this trend.

- **Collaborating with the social partners:** Admitting the social partners into decision-making processes contributes to plans and policies concerning delivery methods, and to the recognition and certification of learning. They are key to qualification systems and may be involved in actual delivery.

📖 *Promoting Adult Learning*, 2005, Chapter 5

Make guidance more ambitious so that it aims to develop career-management skills, as well as providing information to certain groups for immediate decision making: At present, services are largely available to limited numbers of groups, at fixed points in life, focused on immediate decisions. Lifelong learning and active labour market policies call for a wider and more fundamental role in developing career management in all learners and workers through services which are universally accessible throughout the lifespan in ways, locations and at times that reflect diverse client needs.

📖 *Career Guidance and Public Policy: Bridging the Gap*, 2004, Chapter 3

Co-financing is an underpinning principle for adult learners: There is considerable evidence that adult learning benefits adults themselves as well as employers and society. There are different co-financing savings and loan schemes seeking to mirror the way that benefits are shared and to leverage individual contributions with matching contributions provided by the public authorities through individual grants or tax incentives, non-governmental organisations and/or employers. Their success depends on a number of conditions:

- **The creation of new institutional structures for co-financing and a "whole of government"** approach to ensure that public authorities provide more systemic support for financing.

- **Financing schemes need to empower individual learners to choose** what, how, where and when to learn, and where to go with their acquired skills and competences.

- **Government should concentrate its resources on those individuals least able to pay** in times of scarce resources and as the benefits of lifelong learning are widely shared.

- **Co-ordinated policy making** by public authorities and their collaboration with financial institutions, social partners and other stakeholders are required in the implementation of co-financing strategies.

📖 *Co-financing Lifelong Learning: Towards a Systemic Approach*, 2004, Chapters 2 and 3

Exploit the pivotal role of qualifications systems so as to promote dynamic lifelong education and training systems: Certain aspects of qualification systems should receive attention in their implications for lifelong learning implementation, including:

- **Increase flexibility and responsiveness:** Qualifications systems responsive to the changing needs of the economy, employment and the personal ambitions of individuals are "customised", with flexibility promoted by the various mechanisms that increase choice.

- **Facilitate open access to qualifications:** Lifelong learning allows individuals to gain qualifications from different starting points, including the development of new routes to existing qualifications and calling for effective information and guidance systems.

- **Diversify assessment procedures:** Assessment methods and approaches have an important influence on the willingness of individuals to embark on a qualification; credit transfer and outcomes-based methods call for different modes of assessment.

- **Make qualifications progressive:** Accumulating learning experiences and developing competences throughout life represent a significant shift from "once and for all" initial education and training, and call for coherence in the qualifications system.

📖 *Qualifications Systems: Bridges to Lifelong Learning*, 2007, Chapter 2

References

OECD (2004), "Lifelong Learning", *Policy Brief*, OECD Publishing.

OECD (2004), *Career Guidance and Public Policy: Bridging the Gap*, OECD Publishing.

OECD (2004), *Co-financing Lifelong Learning: Towards a Systemic Approach*, OECD Publishing.

OECD (2005), *Promoting Adult Learning*, OECD Publishing.

OECD (2007), *Qualifications Systems: Bridges to Lifelong Learning*, OECD Publishing.

OECD (2007), *Understanding the Brain: The Birth of a Learning Science*, OECD Publishing.

OECD (2010), *Education at a Glance 2010: OECD Indicators*, OECD Publishing.

OECD (2010), *Recognising Non-formal and Informal Learning: Outcomes, Polices and Practices* (by Patrick Werquin), OECD Publishing.

OECD (forthcoming), *Innovative Workplaces: Learning Organisations and Innovation*, OECD Publishing.

6

Outcomes, Benefits and Returns

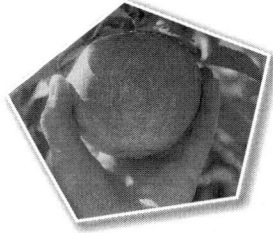

Very rich information on educational outcomes has been generated through OECD work, especially with the triennial Programme for International Student Assessment (PISA), which surveys the achievements of 15-year-olds in reading, mathematics, science and related aspects of competence, together with a range of associated background information. Education is also closely related to employment outcomes and earnings, with key OECD findings reported in this chapter. Additionally there is an expanding analysis of returns to education within the OECD, with findings confirming the positive returns to higher levels of educational attainment on a variety of measures, certainly for the individual, but also for the economy at large. There are also positive returns to early childhood education and care, and to vocational education. Work on the social outcomes of education examines how education influences health, civic participation and social engagement, as well as the economic outcomes.

INTRODUCTION

Very rich information on educational outcomes has been generated through OECD work, especially with the triennial Programme for International Student Assessment (PISA) surveys. These survey the achievement of 15-year-olds in different competence areas, together with a growing range of associated background information, and in many non-member countries and economies, as well as those of the OECD. In charting patterns, large numbers do not attain levels that might be regarded as the minimum for 21st century knowledge economies. There is also expanding analysis of returns to education within the OECD. Findings confirm the positive returns to higher levels of educational attainment on a variety of measures, certainly for the individual, but also for the economy at large. Education affects employment and earnings, but it also has an impact on an individual's well-being and contribution to society. Work on the Social Outcomes of Learning examines the evidence on how education influences health, civic participation and social engagement.

The strong OECD focus on outcomes is set to expand beyond teenage achievements as surveys of adult competences (Programme for the International Assessment of Adult Competencies [PIAAC], see Chapter 5) and outcomes from higher education (Assessment of Higher Education Learning Outcomes [AHELO], see Chapter 4) are in development. The new work on Improving School Outcomes is designed to help countries choose the best tools to assess and improve outcomes.

KEY FINDINGS

Among OECD countries, students in Finland and Korea, with non-members Chinese Taipei and Hong Kong-China, perform above the other countries in mathematics: In these countries in 2006 the mean scores in mathematics were closely grouped between 549 and 547, some way above the next-highest scoring country, the Netherlands (531). Compared with an OECD average of 13.4% attaining the top levels 5 and 6, 27.1% do so in Korea and even more do at 31.9% and 27.7% in Chinese Taipei and Hong Kong-China, respectively. At least one in five students is also proficient in complex mathematics tasks (PISA level 5 or 6) in Belgium, Finland, the Netherlands and Switzerland. In all these countries, there are significant pools of young people with high-level mathematical skills who are likely to play a crucial role in advancing the knowledge economy.

📖 *PISA 2006: Science Competencies for Tomorrow's World: Volume 1: Analysis*, 2007, Chapter 6

Very few countries do not escape having significant minorities, or even a majority, of students with very low performance in mathematics: With the exception of Finland and Korea, all OECD countries have at least 10% of students who achieve at only PISA level 1 or below. In 13 OECD countries (Austria, the Slovak Republic, Hungary, Norway, France, Luxembourg, Spain, the United States, Portugal, Greece, Italy, Turkey, Mexico) this accounts for a fifth or more of the students. The lowest-achieving students in mathematics are actually the majority of 15-year-olds in Mexico (56.5%).

📖 *PISA 2006: Science Competencies for Tomorrow's World: Volume 1: Analysis*, 2007, Chapter 6

In only five OECD countries do more than two-thirds of young people reach or surpass PISA level 3 in reading literacy – the level which involves comprehension and interpretation of moderately complex text: The five countries are Canada, Finland, Ireland, Korea and New Zealand. The average attaining level 3 or above across all OECD countries is 57.1%. Having a high proportion achieving this basic threshold level does not automatically mean that the country has among the highest numbers of top performers: the proportion in Korea attaining the top level 5 (21.7%) is nearly double that achieved in Ireland (11.7%).

📖 *PISA 2006: Science Competencies for Tomorrow's World: Volume 1: Analysis*, 2007, Chapter 6

Figure 6.1.
The spread of student proficiency levels in science in OECD countries (2006)

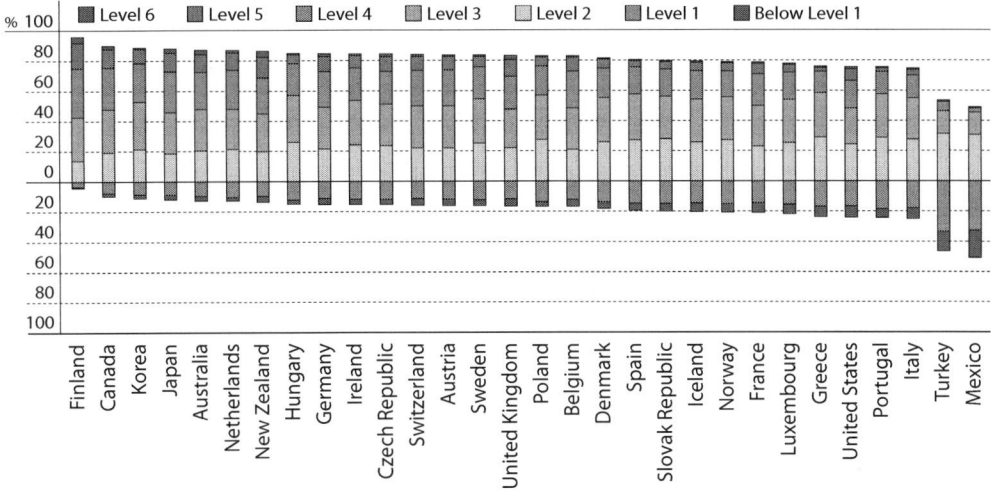

Note: Countries are ranked in descending order of percentages of 15-year-olds at levels 2 and over.
Source: OECD (2007), *PISA 2006: Science Competencies for Tomorrow's World: Volume 1: Analysis*, OECD Publishing.

StatLink http://dx.doi.org/10.1787/141844475532

Figure 6.2.
The spread of student proficiency levels in mathematics in OECD countries (2006)

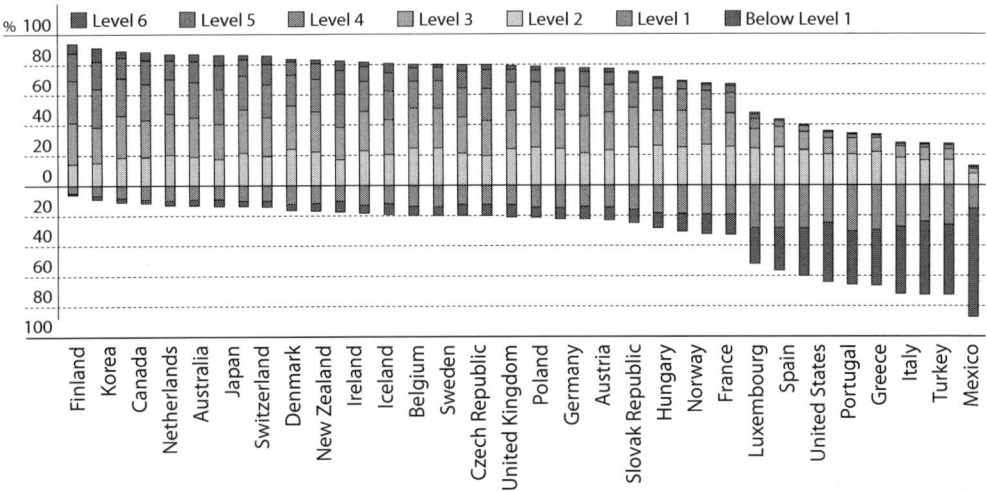

Note: Countries are ranked in descending order of percentages of 15-year-olds at levels 2 and over.
Source: OECD (2007), *PISA 2006: Science Competencies for Tomorrow's World: Volume 1: Analysis*, OECD Publishing.

StatLink http://dx.doi.org/10.1787/142046885031

Figure 6.3.

The spread of student proficiency levels in reading in OECD countries (2006)

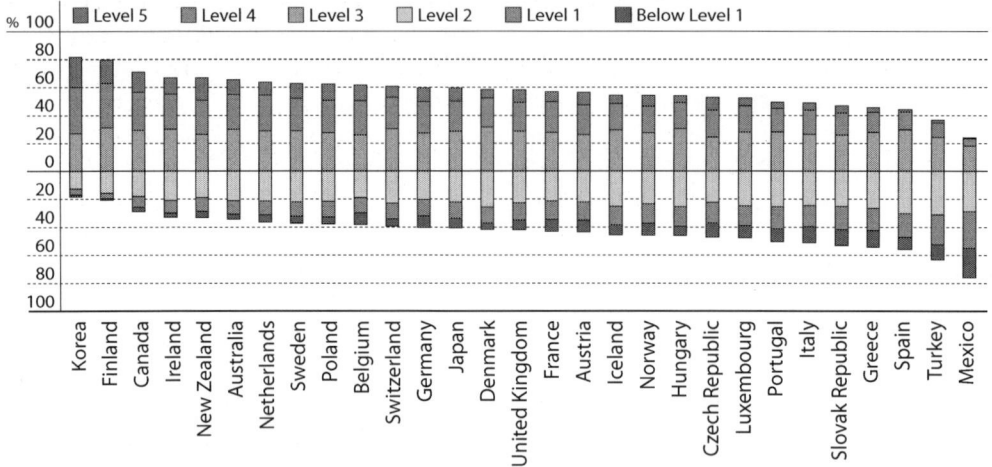

Note: Countries are ranked in descending order of percentages of 15-year-olds at levels 2 and over.
Source: OECD (2007), *PISA 2006: Science Competencies for Tomorrow's World: Volume 1: Analysis,* OECD Publishing.

StatLink http://dx.doi.org/10.1787/142046885031

In 18 OECD countries, 40% or more do not achieve the level 3 threshold in reading literacy, and these low-performing students are the majority in 4 of these countries: The countries which have 40% or more achieving at best at level 2 are Austria, the Czech Republic, Denmark, France, Germany, Japan, Greece, Hungary, Iceland, Italy, Luxembourg, Mexico, Norway, Portugal, the Slovak Republic, Spain, Turkey and the United Kingdom. They are the majority of students in Greece, Italy, Mexico, Portugal, the Slovak Republic, Spain and Turkey.

📖 *PISA 2006: Science Competencies for Tomorrow's World: Volume 1: Analysis,* 2007, Chapter 6

The top performers in science among OECD countries are Finland, followed by Canada, Japan, Korea, New Zealand, Australia and the Netherlands: With OECD countries fixed at an average of 500, the top performer on the combined science scale in 2006 was Finland clearly ahead at 563. Canada (534), Japan, Korea, New Zealand, Australia and the Netherlands (525) are the next group of top-performing OECD countries in science, all at levels 525 and above. On average in these countries, only 1.3% of 15-year-olds reach the top level 6, but in Finland and New Zealand over 3.9% do so. The percentage of these very top science performers is also relatively high (between 2.1% and 2.9%) in Australia, Canada, Japan and the United Kingdom.

📖 *PISA 2006: Science Competencies for Tomorrow's World: Volume 1: Analysis,* 2007, Chapter 2

The gender gap in science performance is small: For most OECD countries there are no statistically significant differences in science performance between young women and men. In six of these countries – Denmark, Luxembourg, Mexico, the Netherlands, Switzerland and the United Kingdom – there is a male advantage, but it is relatively small (between 6 and 10 points). In Turkey and Greece, a somewhat larger female advantage in science (11-12 points) was found in 2006.

📖 *PISA 2006: Science Competencies for Tomorrow's World: Volume 1: Analysis,* 2007, Chapter 2

Investment in early childhood education and care brings significant returns to individuals and society:
Research from diverse countries suggests a common conclusion that investment in young children brings significant benefits not only for children and families, but also for society at large. High quality early childhood services lay a strong foundation of learning which is fundamental to the rest of the lives of the individuals involved. Children from disadvantaged backgrounds, in particular, benefit from acquiring such a foundation. Early childhood investments bring: significant educational, social, economic and labour market returns; improved transitions from one educational level to the next; higher achievement; and lower crime rates among teenagers. Lack of investment in children's services can result in child-care shortages and unequal access, even segregation, of children according to income. Unavailability of services raises barriers against women's full-time employment – with the economic and social consequences which flow from that – and tends to channel women towards low-paid, part-time jobs.

📖 *Starting Strong II: Early Childhood Education and Care*, 2006, Annex D

Attaining at least upper secondary education is an important hedge against the risk of unemployment:
The unemployment rate among those adults aged 25-64 years with an upper secondary education is clearly lower than among those who have not got further than the lower secondary level – on average nearly 4 percentage points lower in 2008. This gap is particular high in the Eastern European OECD countries of the Czech Republic (14 percentage point gap), Hungary (11) and the Slovak Republic (29), and is also high in Germany (9), and in these countries the gap has grown over the past decade. Expressing this upper secondary advantage as a ratio of unemployment rates, those with upper secondary education are half or less than half as likely to be unemployed compared with those with lower secondary education in Austria, the Czech Republic, Germany, Hungary, Norway, the Slovak Republic and Switzerland. There is, however, a group of countries – Chile, Greece, Korea, Luxembourg, Mexico and partner country Brazil – where there is no greater unemployment risk among those finishing education at the lower, compared with the upper secondary, level.

📖 *Education at a Glance 2010: OECD Indicators*, 2010, Indicator A6

In most countries the earnings pay-off for adults having acquired an upper secondary education is clear... but not everywhere: The countries with the highest earnings advantage of those with upper secondary compared with lower secondary education for all working-age adults are Austria, Korea, Portugal, Turkey, the United Kingdom and the United States; in these countries, those with the lower attainments earn around only two-thirds to 70% of upper secondary graduates. The differences can be very marked: Turkish women with lower secondary education earn less than half the incomes of Turkish women with upper secondary education, and in partner country Brazil both men and women with lower secondary education earn only around half of those with upper secondary attainment. There are, however, countries in which the earnings advantage of upper secondary graduates is not particularly marked – the lower attainers earn 90% or more of those with upper secondary education – as is found in Finland for men and women, for men in Belgium, Germany and the partner country Estonia and, for women, in Korea.

📖 *Education at a Glance 2010: OECD Indicators*, 2010, Indicator A7

There is a strong positive relationship between education and the average earnings of individuals, with marked premiums for those with tertiary-level attainments: In all countries, graduates of tertiary education earn substantially more than upper secondary graduates who in turn earn more than those whose attainment does not go beyond basic education. Earnings differentials between higher education and upper secondary graduates are generally greater than between upper and lower secondary graduates. The earnings premium for tertiary over upper secondary graduates, all adult ages and men and women combined, ranges from a high of 2.10 times the incomes of the upper secondary group in Hungary (and 2.54 in partner country Brazil) to a modest 1.18 higher in New Zealand.

📖 *Education at a Glance 2010: OECD Indicators*, 2010, Indicator A7

Figure 6.4.

Relative earnings from employment, by level of educational attainment and gender for 25-64 year-olds (2008 or latest year available)

Upper secondary and post-secondary non-tertiary education = 100

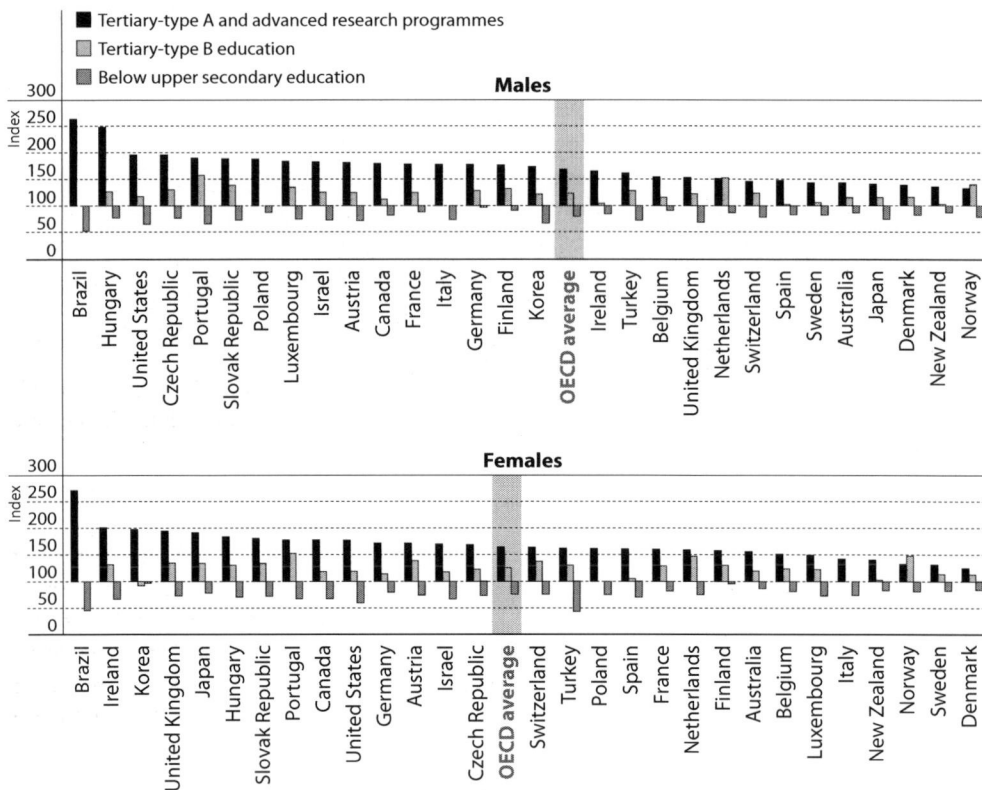

Source: OECD (2010), *Education at a Glance 2010: OECD Indicators*, OECD Publishing.

StatLink ⫯ᵐⁱˢ⌐ http://dx.doi.org/10.1787/888932310206

Even when the additional costs of acquiring more education are taken into account, the higher average subsequent earnings mean that it pays to continue to upper over lower secondary education: For men and women, continuing on to upper secondary education after the lower secondary level pays off on average in all countries. For men, this "private" rate of return stands at 10.6% on average across the 20 OECD countries permitting these calculations, and over 12% in 8 of these countries. The range lies between 4.4% (the Netherlands) and 5.8% (Denmark), to 17.6% (the Czech Republic) and approximately

14% in Australia and Sweden. The range is greater for women, lying between 0.9% in Korea and less than 5% in three countries (Denmark, the Netherlands and New Zealand), up to 20% in the Czech Republic. The average individual rate of return for women for upper secondary education is 9.3%.

📖 *Education at a Glance 2010: OECD Indicators*, 2010, Indicator A8

Though the costs associated with tertiary education can be substantial, they are more than offset by enhanced subsequent average earnings: The relative advantage of continuing on to acquire tertiary over upper secondary education is also positive in all the countries with data, with even larger incentives to continue. For men, it is 11.5% in the 20 countries and 10.7% for women. The rate of return advantage of continuing to tertiary beyond upper secondary rises to 20% or more for men in the Czech Republic and Poland, and to 19% or more for women in the Czech Republic, Poland and Turkey. The countries where the rates of return on higher education are lowest for men and women are Denmark, the Netherlands and Sweden.

📖 *Education at a Glance 2010: OECD Indicators*, 2010, Indicator A8

Projections suggest that there are enormous economic gains to be obtained by OECD countries that can improve the cognitive skills – and not just the educational attainment – of their populations: Projections based on historical relationships (bearing in mind the uncertainties of future projections) suggest that if all OECD countries could boost their average PISA scores by 25 points over the next two decades, the aggregate gain of OECD GDP would be USD 115 trillion over the lifetime of the generation born in 2010. Even more ambitious goals, such as bringing all students to the OECD level of minimal proficiency – a PISA score of 400 – are associated with aggregate GDP increases of nearly USD 200 trillion. Bringing all countries up to the OECD's best performing education system in PISA, Finland, would result in gains in the order of USD 260 trillion. It is the quality of learning outcomes, not the length of schooling, which makes the difference.

📖 *The High Cost of Low Educational Performance: The Long-run Economic Impact of Improving PISA Outcomes*, 2010

Public investment in initial vocational education and training (VET) can make up for insufficient employer provision and delivers good economic returns: Much occupation-specific training is provided by employers but, if left to themselves, they will often not provide their own employees with sufficient training, particularly in transferable skills. Initial VET is designed to fill the gap by providing the needed skills, and research has shown that it can yield good economic returns from the public investment involved. Countries with strong initial VET systems like Germany have been relatively successful in tackling youth unemployment.

📖 *Learning for Jobs*, 2010, Chapter 1

Educational attainment positively enhances health, political interest and trust, with thresholds for the upper secondary level regarding health and for tertiary education with political interest: Adults with higher levels of educational attainment are generally more likely to report that their health is at least good, that they are at least fairly interested in politics, and believe that most people can be trusted. For health, the step in attainment from lower to upper secondary education tends to show up as most influential, while the step up to tertiary is more apparent regarding political interest; no consistent thresholds are apparent regarding trust. The association between education and social outcomes generally remains strong even after adjusting for age, gender and income.

📖 *Education at a Glance 2010: OECD Indicators*, 2010, Indicator A9; *Understanding the Social Outcomes of Learning*, 2007; *Improving Health and Social Cohesion through Education*, forthcoming

Low adult literacy and competency scores are strongly associated with risks of unemployment and insecurity: The first Adult Literacy and Life Skills Survey measured adults' prose, document, numeracy and problem-solving skills across five broad levels of proficiency. Level 3 is identified as the suitable minimum for managing the demands of work and daily life. Based on data gathered from Canada, Italy, Norway, Switzerland, the United States and the Mexican State of Nuevo Leon, as well as Bermuda:

- Individuals whose numeracy scores are at levels 1 and 2 are two to three times more likely to be outside the labour force for six or more months than those with higher scores.
- For young adults, proficiency in document literacy and numeracy is strongly associated with finding employment; young adults scoring at levels 1 and 2 are more likely to stay unemployed for longer periods of time.

📖 *Learning a Living: First Results of the Adult Literacy and Life Skills Survey*, 2005

Training enhances wages and job prospects, especially for younger, mobile and highly-educated workers: Adult education and training have a significant impact on both worker productivity and wage levels. Diverse national and international panel studies (altogether covering 13 European countries and the United States) have come up with wage premiums resulting from participation in training courses ranging from negligible in France to 2.5% annually in Germany and 5% in Portugal. Training tends also to reduce the chance of being unemployed and increases chances of reemployment in the case of lay-off. The wage gains associated with the training are improved when workers move on from their employers; the higher premiums come from learning taken with previous employers and with the best results for young and highly-educated workers.

📖 *Promoting Adult Learning*, 2005, Chapter 2; *OECD Employment Outlook 2004*, 2004, Chapter 4

Recognition of non-formal and informal learning delivers economic, educational, social and psychological benefits: Recognition of non-formal and informal learning generates economic benefits: it reduces both the costs associated with, and the time required to acquire qualifications in, formal education. It also allows human capital to be deployed more productively by giving people access to jobs that better match their true skills. Recognition provides educational benefits by helping people learn about themselves and develop their career within a lifelong learning framework. It provides social benefits by improving equity through giving access to further education and the labour market to disadvantaged minority groups, disaffected youth, and older workers who missed out on education earlier. Recognition can provide psychological benefits by making people aware of their capabilities and offering external validation of their worth.

📖 *Recognising Non-formal and Informal Learning: Outcomes, Policies and Practices*, 2010, Executive Summary

POLICY DIRECTIONS

Education needs to re-invent itself in order to improve the performance of systems and to raise value for money: This will be a tremendous challenge for public policy. It will require often supply-driven education systems to develop effective mechanisms to understand and respond to rapidly-changing economic and social demands for competencies. Effective policies will require understanding not just of the development of competencies, but also of how effectively economies use their talent pool, and of how competencies in turn feed into better jobs, higher productivity, and positive economic and social outcomes. The success of education systems will be measured less by how much countries spend on education or how many complete a degree, and more by the educational outcomes achieved and by their impact on economic and social progress.

📖 *Education at a Glance 2010: OECD Indicators*, 2010, Editorial

Foster student interest in science, mathematics and technology education as an explicit objective:
Recognising that a declining interest in science, mathematics and technology studies is of particular
concern in many countries, and considering that students' motivation and engagement in these
areas closely relate to their achievement and potentially to their future career choices, the OECD
encourages educational policies and practices that foster students' interest and engagement in science,
mathematics and technology. Considering the strong association between gender differences in
interest and motivation in science-related areas at school and subsequent patterns of educational and
career pathways, the OECD also suggests to place greater emphasis on engaging female students in
these subject areas.

📖 *Education Policy Analysis 2006: Focus on Higher Education*, 2006, Chapter 5

Countries should aim to secure similar student performance among schools: Low "between-school
variation" means that there is no obvious advantage in terms of performance for a student to attend one
school as opposed to another – they all perform to broadly equal levels. In three countries – Norway,
Finland and Iceland – less than 10% of variation in mathematics achievement in 2003 was accounted for
by such differences – all the rest of the variation is "within-school". The OECD average is much higher
than 10% and stands at almost exactly a third. The countries where it is over 60% are Turkey, Hungary
and Japan. Securing similar student performance among schools is both important in itself as a policy
goal and is compatible with high overall performance standards.

📖 *Education at a Glance 2006: OECD Indicators*, 2006, Indicator A5

**Clarify returns to training by augmenting information and removing structural barriers, and
by making the outcomes more transparent to individuals and firms:** Effective dissemination of
information can help convince individuals and firms of the benefits of training. Cost/benefit analysis
provides information that can encourage and motivate adults to learn, as well as clarifying who should
cover the financial costs. Efforts to stimulate firms to invest in training would be assisted by promoting
the transparency of human capital investments in company accounting. Acting directly on increasing
the returns to training through alternative mechanisms, such as embedding skill improvements in the
wage determination process, can improve training take-up and firm productivity. The development of
national qualifications systems provides a sort of currency in this respect and recognition of informal
and non-formal learning contributes to reducing the opportunity cost of learning.

📖 *Promoting Adult Learning*, 2005, Chapter 2

References

OECD (2004), *OECD Employment Outlook 2004*, OECD Publishing.

OECD (2005), *Promoting Adult Learning*, OECD Publishing.

OECD (2006), *Starting Strong II: Early Childhood Education and Care*, OECD Publishing.

OECD (2006), *Education at a Glance 2006: OECD Indicators*, OECD Publishing.

OECD (2006), *Education Policy Analysis 2006: Focus on Higher Education*, OECD Publishing.

OECD (2007), *PISA 2006: Science Competencies for Tomorrow's World: Volume 1: Analysis*, OECD Publishing.

OECD (2007), *Understanding the Social Outcomes of Learning*, OECD Publishing.

OECD (2010), *Recognising Non-formal and Informal Learning: Outcomes, Polices and Practices* (by Patrick Werquin), OECD Publishing.

OECD (2010), *The High Cost of Low Educational Performance: The Long-run Economic Impact of Improving PISA Outcomes* (by Erik A. Hanushek and Ludger Woessmann), OECD Publishing.

OECD (2010), *Education at a Glance 2010: OECD Indicators*, OECD Publishing.

OECD (2010), *Learning for Jobs*, OECD Publishing.

OECD (forthcoming), *Improving Health and Social Cohesion through Education*, OECD Publishing.

Statistics Canada and OECD (2005), *Learning a Living: First Results of the Adult Literacy and Life Skills Survey*, OECD Publishing.

7

Equity and Equality of Opportunity

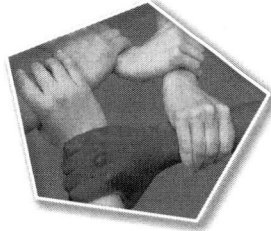

Analyses of developments and policies that influence equity have been an underlying priority in much of the OECD educational work. The persistent patterns of inequality have been highlighted, with the increasing quality of international data permitting analyses relating to many pertinent groups of learners and their educational experiences. The dimensions and groups include gender, age, migrant status, special needs and social background, and cover adult formal and non-formal learning, as well as schooling, vocational education and higher education. Recent OECD analysis has also charted the nature of the "digital divide". Findings and recommendations from a major international review of equity in education published in 2007 – No More Failures *– are presented. The chapter reports promising policy directions from studies published since then, including those on immigrants' education, cultural diversity and teacher education, and on adults in foundation programmes for numeracy and literacy.*

INTRODUCTION

Analyses of developments and policies that influence equity have been an underlying priority in much of the OECD educational work. The persistent patterns of inequality have been highlighted, with the increasing quality of international data permitting analyses relating to many pertinent groups of learners and their educational experiences. OECD analysis has shown that there need be no contradiction between equity and efficiency, and indeed has underlined how damaging to economic as well as social goals is the phenomenon of exclusion and widespread under-achievement. A major international review of equity in education – *No More Failures,* published in 2007 – outlines ten broad policy directions around the design of provision, practices and resourcing. The charting of the outcomes of, and opportunities and policies for, different population groups has been undertaken across the many sectors of education and training, including longstanding work on special educational needs.

Ethnic and cultural diversity makes society richer, but reaping the full benefits requires special efforts from the education system. The OECD *Thematic Reviews on Migrant Education* have examined the education outcomes of the children of immigrants in five OECD countries. Diversity in the classroom can enhance learning and prepare students for the outside world but major challenges are facing many schools and teachers to make this happen; the "Teacher Education for Diversity" project examines how countries educate teachers to respond to increasing cultural diversity and the educational challenges faced by indigenous populations. Language is one key to success and work on Globalisation and Linguistic Competencies explores why some individuals are successful in learning non-native languages and others not, and why certain education systems appear more successful than others at teaching non-native languages.

KEY FINDINGS

There is no contradiction between equity and efficiency in education: There is a widespread argument that the redistribution of resources to those in greatest need helps equity but damages efficiency. The OECD in its analysis of equity, as well as the World Bank, argue that equity and efficiency are in fact complementary. This is clearly the case within basic education: school failure has large costs not only to those involved, but also to society, because the welfare costs of marginalised persons are large. Reasonably-priced, effective measures to address failure benefit both efficiency and equity. Some analyses even suggest that an equitable distribution of skills across populations has a strong impact on overall economic performance.

📖 *No More Failures: Ten Steps to Equity in Education*, 2007, Chapter 1; World Bank, 2005

The countries with high quality and high equity have embraced student heterogeneity and avoided premature and differentiated structures: Early tracking is associated with reduced equity in outcomes and sometimes weakens results overall. In countries with early selection of students into highly differentiated education systems, differences among schools are large and the relationship between socio-economic background and student school performance stronger.

📖 *No More Failures: Ten Steps to Equity in Education*, 2007, Chapter 3

The general upgrading of attainments and qualifications increasingly excludes those who have not shared in this advance: Many adults remain unqualified and some young people still do not successfully complete secondary education. Across the OECD nearly one in three adults (31%) have only primary or lower secondary education – a real disadvantage in terms of employment and life chances. In all OECD countries, those with weak basic qualifications are much less likely to continue learning in adult life and there are big differences between countries. That there are fewer proportionately with these very low attainment and qualification levels increases the risk of their exclusion and detachment from economic and social life.

📖 *No More Failures: Ten Steps to Equity in Education*, 2007, Chapter 2

Choice may stimulate quality but with risks for equity: There are quality arguments to be made in favour of creating a degree of choice as a vehicle for stimulating improvement. When choices exist, schools must then look beyond their own walls at what others – their potential "competitors" – are doing; without some room for exit to be exercised, parents and students have no threat to back up voice. OECD work confirms that better educated, middle-class parents are more likely to avail themselves of choice opportunities and send their children to the "best" school they can find, widening the gaps between the sought-after schools and the rest. Across countries, greater choice in school systems is associated with larger differences in the social composition of different schools.

📖 *No More Failures: Ten Steps to Equity in Education*, 2007, Chapter 3; *Demand-sensitive Schooling? Evidence and Issues*, 2006

Figure 7.1.

Women have overtaken men in upper secondary and higher education: Attainments of different adult age groups, 2008

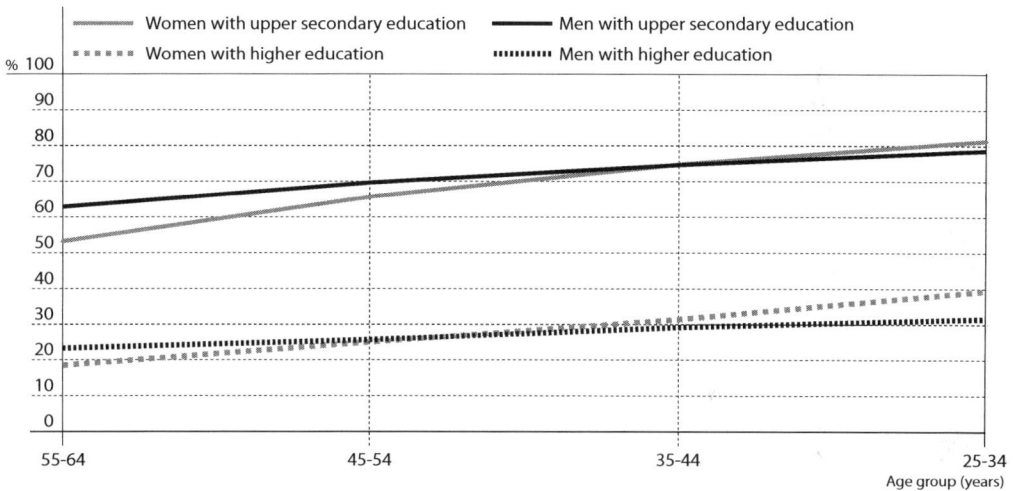

Source: *OECD Education Database.*

StatLink ⌖ http://dx.doi.org/10.1787/888932310092

Girls and women have now moved clearly ahead of boys and men in education: The number of expected years in education between ages 15 and 29 across OECD countries enjoyed by young women – 6.9 years – now surpasses those of young men who average only 6.7. It was higher in all OECD countries in 2008 except Australia, Germany, Japan, Luxembourg, Mexico, the Netherlands, New Zealand, Switzerland and Turkey. Female graduation rates from upper secondary education are higher in 23 of the 26 OECD countries permitting the comparison – the exceptions being Switzerland, Turkey and the United States, as well as in all of the partner countries for which such comparisons could be made. The female advantage gap is more than ten percentage points in Denmark, Iceland, New Zealand, Norway, Portugal, Slovenia and Spain. Moreover, only in Japan, Korea, Switzerland and Turkey do the entry rates of men to tertiary education now exceed those of women.

📖 *Education at a Glance 2010: OECD Indicators*, 2010, Indicators A2 and C3

Recent PISA analyses have identified three groups of countries regarding gender differences in science performance across countries and within schools:

- **Where gender differences are insignificant on the three competency scales of science performance and within schools:** examples here are Australia, Finland, Iceland, Ireland, Japan, Korea, New Zealand, Norway, Sweden and the partner country Estonia.

- **Where there is an insignificant overall gender difference but those within schools in favour of male students are significant:** Belgium, Czech Republic, France, Germany, Hungary, Italy, the Slovak Republic, (as well as the partner countries/economies Croatia, Hong Kong-China, Macao-China, Montenegro, Romania, Serbia, Tunisia, Uruguay).

- **Where there are consistently high gender differences in favour of males, on both the overall science score and within schools:** examples of these, before and after accounting for programme level and destination, are Denmark, Luxembourg and the United Kingdom.

📖 *Equally Prepared for Life? How 15-Year-Old Boys and Girls Perform in School,* 2009, Chapter 4

Relatively small proportions of compulsory school students receive additional funding for their education due to special needs, though there are cases where this amounts to 1 in 5 students: In the countries supplying data on additional funding across the three categories of needs (disabilities, difficulties and disadvantages), nearly 3% median of students (2.7%) receive additional outlays because they are assessed as disabled, rising to just over 5% in the United States. Additional spending on those with difficulties is in general low (2.4%), rising to 3.3% for those counted as "disadvantaged". Much higher proportions are found in some countries – such as the 17% of United Kingdom compulsory students qualifying for funding due to learning difficulties, the 15% and over in the Flemish Community of Belgium, Mexico, the Netherlands and the United States because of their disadvantage.

📖 *Students with Disabilities, Learning Difficulties and Disadvantages: Policies, Statistics and Indicators – 2007 Edition,* 2008, Chapter 4

Boys with disabilities and receiving additional resources outnumber such girls by approximately 60 to 40, rising to two-thirds to one-third in their call on specific resources for learning and behavioural difficulties: These are consistent results, repeatedly found in different studies with different methodologies. There is a consistent majority of males over females in special needs education provision or in receipt of additional resources for disabilities and learning difficulties. Whether looked at by location (special school, special class, regular class), cross-nationally or nationally, age of student or stage of education, boys outnumber girls. For learning difficulties, the difference is even larger with males outnumbering females by two-thirds to one-third.

📖 *Students with Disabilities, Learning Difficulties and Disadvantages: Policies, Statistics and Indicators – 2007 Edition,* 2008, Chapter 4

The digital divide defined by technology access has faded in schools but a second one based on digital competence more stubbornly remains: In almost all OECD countries, students attend schools equipped with computers and most of these are connected to the Internet (though there do remain some gaps in digital home access). A more stubborn digital divide is that between those who have the necessary competences and skills to benefit from computer use, and those who do not, which competences are closely linked to students' economic, cultural and social capital. Nevertheless, school use of digital media can help to reduce the digital divide, and computer use is associated with improved academic skills and competences.

📖 *Are the New Millennium Learners Making the Grade? Technology Use and Educational Performance in PISA,* 2010, Chapters 4, 5 and Executive Summary

Figure 7.2.

Proportion of 20-24 year-olds who are not in education and have not attained upper secondary education, by migrant status (2007)

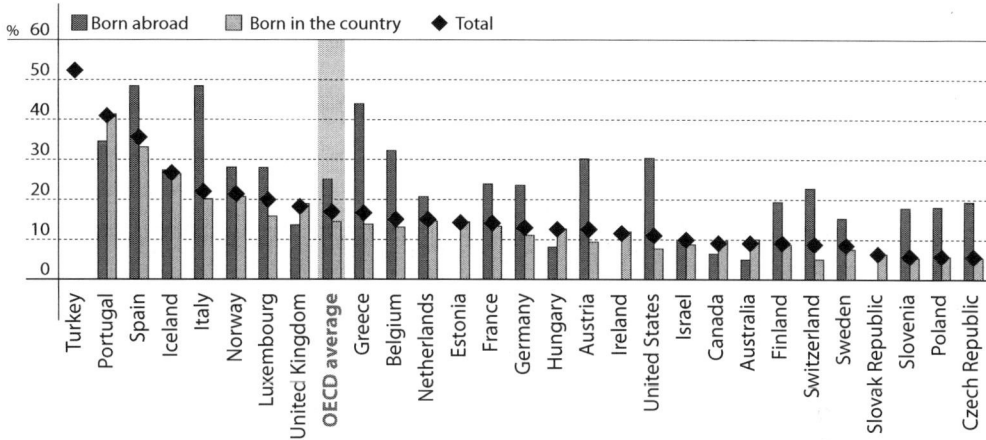

Source: OECD (2010), *Education at a Glance 2010: OECD Indicators*, OECD Publishing.

StatLink ⬛ᵢᵢₛ🖳 http://dx.doi.org/10.1787/888932310453

Immigrant students largely face greater difficulties in education than their native peers: The performance of immigrant students in reading, science and mathematics in compulsory education is for the most part comparatively lower than that of their native peers. This is despite generally positive attitudes towards learning among immigrant students. In some countries immigrant students (first-generation) are less likely to attend early childhood education and care institutions, and more likely to repeat a grade, attend vocational schools and drop out from secondary education. They have more limited access to quality education. They are more likely to attend schools that are located in big cities that serve students who are on average from less advantaged socio-economic backgrounds and with higher concentrations of other immigrant students.

📖 *Closing the Gap for Immigrant Students: Policies, Practice, and Performance*, 2010, Chapter 2; *Where Immigrant Students Succeed: A Comparative Review of Performance and Engagement in PISA 2003*, 2006, Chapter 2

Young adults born abroad are much more likely than the others to be already out of education and not to have completed upper secondary education (but with notable exceptions): Many more young adults aged 20-24 years old have low educational attainment – as indicated by having already left education without having completed at the least upper secondary education – when they are born outside the country (see Figure 7.2). Across the OECD, a quarter of this age group born abroad has low attainment on this measure as compared with only 15% of those born in the country. The gap is 20 percentage points or more in Austria, Greece, Italy and the United States. Yet, not everywhere do immigrant young adults lag behind the rest of the population in educational attainment: a higher proportion of foreign-born 20-24 year-olds are still in education or already have upper secondary education in Australia, Canada, Hungary, Portugal and the United Kingdom than those born in the country.

📖 *Education at a Glance 2010: OECD Indicators*, 2010, Indicator C3

Top performers in science generally attend schools with relatively privileged students and often private, though in some systems the link to social background is weaker: Top performers in science at age 15 tend to be in schools where others are also high performers and from relatively advantaged socio-economic backgrounds. Many such schools select students according to their academic record and many of them are private. Typically, about a quarter of top performers in science come from a socio-economic background below the country's average but in Japan, Finland and Austria, and the partner economies Macao-China and Hong Kong-China, a third or more of the top performers in science come from such a lower socio-economic background. Female students are as likely to be top performers as male students.

📖 *Top of the Class: High Performers in Science in PISA 2006*, 2009, Chapter 2

Socially advantaged and female students spend more time in regular lessons and individual study in science, mathematics and the language of instruction: In most countries, socio-economically advantaged students spend much more time in regular school lessons and individual study in science, mathematics and the language of instruction than disadvantaged students: about 11.5 hours per week studying those 3 subjects in regular school lessons compared with 9.8 hours per week for disadvantaged students. This overall OECD difference of 1 hour and 42 minutes per week breaks down into around 50 minutes more per week in science, 30 minutes more mathematics and 20 minutes in the language of instruction. In most countries, females spend around 40 minutes more time in regular school lessons and individual study in science, mathematics and the language of instruction than males.

📖 *Quality Time for Students: Learning In and Out of School*, forthcoming, Chapter 3

In many OECD countries, tertiary education remains dominated by students from well-educated backgrounds: Evidence from the 1990s showed that young people whose parents had tertiary education themselves were between two and six times as likely to complete tertiary studies as those whose parents had only secondary level qualifications. Only a few countries have data to permit such calculations; among that do, students with fathers who had completed higher education were more than twice as likely to be in higher education in Austria, France, Germany, Portugal and the United Kingdom. It is substantially less in Spain (1.5 as likely) and Ireland (1.1). Countries providing more equal access to higher education – such as Finland, Ireland and Spain – are also the countries with the more equal between-school performances in PISA 2000.

📖 *No More Failures: Ten Steps to Equity in Education*, 2007; *Education at a Glance 2007: OECD Indicators*, 2007, Indicator A7

Social background strongly influences teenage expectations to go on to complete higher education, with the influence seen most powerfully in the Slovak Republic, Switzerland and Hungary: PISA information on students' social backgrounds allow their categorisation into "high" and "low" socio-economic status, and the comparison between the expectations of the "high" group of 15-year-olds to complete higher education and the expectations of the "low" group. In all countries, there is a clear relationship between expectations to get an advanced education and social background, with the odds mainly in the range of 2.0 to 2.9. The odds are lowest – expectations least shaped by background – in Finland (1.8). They are over 2.9 in Austria (3.0), Belgium (3.0), Greece (3.0), the Slovak Republic (3.1) and Switzerland (3.1), and rise to 4.0 in Hungary.

📖 *Education at a Glance 2007: OECD Indicators*, 2007, Indicator A4

Engagement in adult learning is far higher among those already well qualified compared with those with low attainment, as it is for younger compared with older adults: On average across OECD countries, someone with tertiary education is almost three times as likely to be involved in some form of formal or non-formal adult learning programme as those with only low attainment levels. It is even around 20 percentage points higher than those with the upper secondary level attainment. In countries where adult learning is widespread these gaps tend to be less marked. The gaps among women tend to be wider than for men according to background education: female tertiary graduates engage more in adult learning than male tertiary graduates, but women with low educational attainment lag behind even the poorly qualified men. Older adults (55-64 year-olds) are half as likely to engage in adult education activities as younger adults (25-34 year-olds).

📖 *Education at a Glance 2010: OECD Indicators,* 2010, Indicator A5

Recognition of non-formal and informal learning outcomes addresses equity by offering additional opportunities and routes for those who otherwise miss out: First, it can make it easier for dropouts to return to formal learning, giving them a second chance. Second, it can be attractive to groups such as indigenous people and migrants whose competences may otherwise be less recognised, or who have not been able to acquire qualifications through the formal education system. Third, it can help to rebalance equity between generations since a much smaller cohort of older workers had access to higher education and its qualifications than is the case today.

📖 *Recognising Non-formal and Informal Learning: Outcomes, Policies and Practices,* 2010, Executive Summary

POLICY DIRECTIONS

The OECD advances ten steps – major policy recommendations which would reduce school failure and dropout, make society fairer and avoid the large social costs of marginalised adults with few basic skills. These include:

1. **Limit early tracking and streaming, and postpone academic selection:** The OECD suggests careful review of early differentiation into schools of different types in those education systems that practise it and holds strong reservations about introducing it in those education systems that do not. The early tracking and streaming of school students need to be justified in terms of proven benefits, given that it so often poses a risk to equity. Systems that use early tracking should consider raising the age when it first takes place and academic selection needs to be used with caution.

2. **Manage school choice so as to contain the risks to equity:** The exercise of choice poses risks to equity and requires careful management to ensure that it does not increase the differences in social composition of different schools. When there is the exercise of parental choice, the oversubscribed schools need to find ways to even out the social mix – such as through lottery systems as selection methods – and financial premiums to schools with disadvantaged students may also help.

3. **In upper secondary education, provide attractive alternatives, remove dead ends and prevent dropout:** Early prevention of dropout is the best cure and monitoring those at risk should be linked to interventions to improve outcomes and prevent dropout. Basic schooling should support those who are struggling rather than focus primarily on those who excel. Upper secondary education should be attractive, offering good quality pathways with effective links to the world of work. Special programmes to smooth transitions at the end of basic schooling can help encourage students to stay in school. Good quality vocational tracks are essential – removing an academic hurdle from entrance to general upper secondary education, as Norway and Sweden have done, can serve to increase the status of vocational tracks.

4. **Offer second chances to gain from education:** Second chances are necessary for those who lack basic education and skills. These include programmes that provide literacy training, primary and secondary education, work-based programmes and arrangements to recognise informal learning. Across OECD countries, many adults and young dropouts without basic education obtain school qualifications through second chance programmes. In the United States, almost 60% of dropouts eventually earn a high school credential (GED certificate).

5. **Provide systematic help to those who fall behind in school and reduce high rates of school-year repetition:** The high repetition rates in some countries should be reduced by changing incentives to schools so that they do not so readily use repetition and through developing alternatives for those who are struggling. One way is through greater interventions in classrooms which have proved to be effective in addressing learning needs of weaker students, like the Finnish approach of offering a sequence of intensifying interventions for those with difficulties to draw them back into the mainstream. Teachers need a highly-developed professional repertoire aimed at supporting those who are falling behind.

6. **Strengthen the links between school and home, especially for disadvantaged families:** Parental involvement – working with children at home and actively participating in school activities – improves results. Disadvantaged parents tend to be among the least involved: schools need to target their efforts to improve communication with the most disadvantaged parents and help develop environments conducive to learning in homes. After-school homework clubs offer one way to support those with weak home support.

7. **Respond to diversity and provide for the successful inclusion of migrants and minorities within mainstream education:** Incentives to encourage immigrants into early childhood education are important. Particular attention needs to be given to language learning at all levels, including through teacher professional development – for this and for all other aspects of teaching in multicultural environments. At the same time, segregation must be avoided including the tendency for too many immigrant children to end up in special education institutions.

8. **Provide strong education for all, giving priority to early childhood provision and basic schooling:** Where fees are involved in early childhood education, they should be moderate and remitted for those too poor to pay. Countries which charge fees for early childhood but not tertiary education need to re-examine their policies on equity grounds. A strong focus is needed in basic education on those with learning difficulties, and the implicit incentive for some to drop out provided by linking grants to families with school performance means that this practice should be reviewed on equity grounds.

9. **Direct resources to the students with the greatest needs, so that poorer communities enjoy at least the same level of provision as others better-off, and to support schools in difficulty:** Countries need adequate mechanisms to redistribute resources and minimise regional inequities in provision with the aim of reaching acceptable minimum standards everywhere. Additional resources need to be channelled through schools to help disadvantaged students while the stigma of labelling particular schools as "for disadvantaged students" should be avoided.

10. **Set concrete targets for more equity, particularly related to low school attainment and dropouts:** Numerical targets are a useful policy lever through articulating clearly what is to be achieved, rather than simply the means to improvement. Countries can usefully adopt a small number of

numerical targets, particularly for reducing the numbers of school-leavers with poor basic skills and of early school dropouts. Policy needs also to manage, and respond to, the public debate which follows publication of school-level test results, so that it does not exacerbate the equity problems themselves, and it should give energetic support to those schools with weak results.

📖 *No More Failures: Ten Steps to Equity in Education*, 2007, Summary and Policy Recommendations

Many of the factors involved in improving teaching and teacher education for cultural diversity are identical with good practice in general; others are specific to the challenges of diversity:

- **Develop a shared vision on the nature of increasingly diverse populations,** at different levels and with a variety of stakeholders on how these are reflected in schools and classrooms, and how to accommodate changing landscapes.

- **Improve the diversity of student teachers and teachers,** calling for holistic policy plans within countries and regions for attracting, retaining and inserting diverse student teachers into the teaching force.

- **Promote awareness of contextual specificity and preparation for teaching diverse student populations in pre-service and in-service teacher programmes,** from general principles of working in diverse educational contexts to teaching specific student populations.

- **Focus on improving the attraction and retention of diverse student teachers and teachers,** who can serve as important role models and bring different perspectives into the classroom.

- **Focus on attracting and retaining well-qualified teachers in diverse schools,** understanding better how to do it and implementing necessary measures.

- **Encourage timely, relevant and coherent data collection about who is in the diverse classroom landscape** for more informed decision making on how best to respond.

📖 *Educating Teachers for Diversity: Meeting the Challenge*, 2010, Chapter 13

Actively engaging immigrant parents and communities in education represents an important goal in improving equity, with many promising examples of how this can be done: Parental and community involvement involving immigrant groups and families represent key directions for building positive attitudes and conditions for achievement, as well as enriching school systems. Among the promising directions being followed and programmes established in different countries and localities are:

- Providing adequate information through various communication channels.

- Establishing partnerships between schools and parents.

- Building national platforms for immigrant parents.

- Involving parents in early childhood education and care.

- Involving parents in classroom instruction.

- Assisting and up-skilling immigrant parents.

- Setting up "ethnic mentoring/role models" programmes.

- Encouraging community involvement in providing opportunities for young immigrants.

- Providing additional learning time and after-school support.

📖 *Closing the Gap for Immigrant Students: Policies, Practice and Performance*, 2010, Chapter 3

The OECD has identified seven interrelated areas where policy can do more to help strengthen and develop effective practice, and improve outcomes for adults who need education to address foundation skills in language, literacy and numeracy (LLN):

- **Promote active debate on the nature of teaching, learning and assessment:** Countries need open discussion about such questions as what should be the underlying principles driving provision in the adult LLN system, and what counts as success and for whom?

- **Strengthen professionalism:** Effective teaching, learning and assessment hinge on the quality of interactions between and among educators and learners; countries will need to continue to strengthen practice through rigorous qualification and professional development requirements.

- **Balance structure and flexibility – formative assessment as a framework:** Policies should include the development of broadly-defined learning objectives, tools for community-based and work-based programmes, guidelines on the process and the principles of formative assessment, as well as appropriate professional development.

- **Strengthen learner-centred approaches:** To ensure that learners' needs are diagnosed and addressed, individual motivations, interests and goals are incorporated into teaching, and learners may choose whether or not to pursue qualifications.

- **Diversify and deepen approaches to programme evaluation for accountability:** Given the range of stakeholder interests, no single approach can satisfy all needs. Systems that use diverse, well-aligned measures of learning processes, as well as outcomes, will be better able to manage competing goals and interests, and to capture useful data.

- **Devote the necessary resources of people, time and money:** The fragile funding and voluntary nature of much LLN provision often impedes the goals of professionalising the field and improving outcomes.

- **Strengthen the knowledge base:** There is a very large research agenda as the knowledge base remains seriously under-developed; this should include evaluations of promising teaching and assessment practices, policies and implementation, and it will need to pay much greater attention to impact.

📖 *Teaching, Learning and Assessment for Adults: Improving Foundation Skills*, 2008, Chapter 11

References

OECD (2006), *Where Immigrant Students Succeed: A Comparative Review of Performance and Engagement in PISA 2003*, OECD Publishing.

OECD (2006), *Demand-sensitive Schooling? Evidence and Issues,* OECD Publishing.

OECD (2007), *No More Failures: Ten Steps to Equity in Education* (by Simon Field, Malgorzata Kuczera and Beatriz Pont), OECD Publishing.

OECD (2007), *Education at a Glance 2007: OECD Indicators,* OECD Publishing.

OECD (2008), *Students with Disabilities, Learning Difficulties and Disadvantages: Policies, Statistics and Indicators – 2007 Edition,* OECD Publishing.

OECD (2008), *Teaching, Learning and Assessment for Adults: Improving Foundation Skills* (edited by Janet Looney), OECD Publishing.

OECD (2009), *Equally Prepared for Life? How 15-Year-Old Boys and Girls Perform in School,* OECD Publishing.

OECD (2009), *Top of the Class: High Performers in Science in PISA 2006,* OECD Publishing.

OECD (2010), *Are the New Millennium Learners Making the Grade? Technology Use and Educational Performance in PISA*, OECD Publishing.

OECD (2010), *Educating Teachers for Diversity: Meeting the Challenge,* OECD Publishing.

OECD (2010), *Recognising Non-formal and Informal Learning: Outcomes, Polices and Practices* (by Patrick Werquin), OECD Publishing.

OECD (2010), *Education at a Glance 2010: OECD Indicators,* OECD Publishing.

OECD (2010), *Closing the Gap for Immigrant Students: Policies, Practice and Performance*, OECD Publishing.

OECD (forthcoming), *Quality Time for Students: Learning In and Out of School*, OECD Publishing.

World Bank (2005), *World Development Report 2006,* World Bank and Oxford University Press.

8

INNOVATION AND KNOWLEDGE MANAGEMENT

Recognition of the key role of research and knowledge management in educational practice and policy making is in general recent. The volume of relevant educational research and development (R&D) tends to be low, despite education being so explicitly about knowledge, and there has been only weak capacity to develop and exploit the knowledge base on which to build improved practice and effective policies. A great deal of educational change is still shaped by short-term considerations despite education's fundamental long-term mission and nature. Improving the knowledge base and fostering innovation have been the aims of policy in a number of countries. Within the OECD, analyses of educational R&D systems, knowledge management, innovative practice and systemic innovation, futures thinking, and evidence-informed policy and practice, have all been prominent, some of it carried out in contribution to the OECD's horizontal Innovation Strategy. Analysis has also focused around the so-called 21st century skills, seen as fundamental to innovative and creative societies.

INTRODUCTION

Innovation is a longstanding focus of educational work at the OECD: the Centre for Educational Research and Innovation (CERI) was founded over 40 years ago in 1968. Most recently, this Centre has provided the educational contribution to the OECD-wide "Innovation Strategy", which is also looking at other sectors such as entrepreneurship, science, technology, research, immigration, tax and trade in order to help countries capture the economic benefits of innovation. Work on "New Millennium Learners" has focused especially on how education systems can best use and develop the skills for technology, including through technology-rich innovation. The "Innovative Learning Environments" project is compiling examples of innovations that reconfigure the way that learning takes place.

Recognition of the key role of research and knowledge management in educational practice and policy making has been growing but still tends to be weakly developed. In many countries, there has been only limited capacity to develop and exploit the knowledge base on which improved practice and effective policies can be based. The volume of relevant educational R&D tends generally to be low, despite education being so explicitly about knowledge. Similarly, a great deal of educational change is still shaped by short-term considerations despite education's fundamental long-term mission and nature. Educational R&D systems, knowledge management, futures thinking, and evidence-informed policy and practice, have all been prominent aspects of the research and innovation work of the OECD in education.

KEY FINDINGS

For a person, organisation, economy or society to be innovative requires wide-ranging skills, including "soft skills", making it a priority to ask how effectively education systems foster them: Innovation covers a wide range of activities, from invention and breakthroughs, to implementation and minor improvements. It therefore necessitates a wide variety of skills:

- **Basic skills and digital age literacy:** These include reading, writing and numeracy, and the skills to use digital technology, and to access and interpret information.

- **Academic skills:** Associated with disciplines such as languages, mathematics, history, law and science, these skills are generally obtained through the education system and are transferable across different situations.

- **Technical skills:** The specific skills needed in an occupation, which may include both academic and vocational skills, as well as knowledge of certain tools or processes.

- **Generic skills:** Skills of this sort commonly are seen to include problem-solving, critical and creative thinking, ability to learn, and ability to manage complexity. A skill such as problem solving may be considered as transferable, but some argue that it is also firm-specific.

- **"Soft" skills:** These include working in teams and heterogeneous groups, communication, motivation, volition and initiative, the ability to read and manage one's own and others' emotions and behaviours, multicultural openness, and receptiveness to innovation.

- **Leadership:** Related to "soft" skills, these include team building and steering, coaching and mentoring, lobbying and negotiating, co-ordination, ethics and charisma.

📖 *The OECD Innovation Strategy: Getting a Head Start on Tomorrow*, 2010, Chapter 3

Schools are conventionally poor at using the key motors of innovation – research knowledge, networking, modular restructuring, technological advance: OECD work on knowledge management has identified four key "pumps of innovation":

- **The "science-based" innovation pump:** Education has not traditionally made enough direct use of research knowledge, and there is often cultural resistance to doing so. This is increasingly being targeted in reform.

- **The "horizontally-organised" innovation pump:** There are obvious benefits in terms of teachers pooling their knowledge through networks, but incentives to do so remain underdeveloped. There is need to tighten the "loose coupling" between the single teachers, individual classrooms and individual schools that so characterise school systems.

- **The "modular structures" pump:** This is about building complex processes from smaller sub-systems that are designed independently, but function together. Education is accustomed to working in modules, but much of it involves schools or teachers operating separately from each other.

- **The "information and communication technologies"** (ICT) pump: There is a powerful potential for ICT to transform education, but its use in schools remains underdeveloped, partly because the main *modus operandi* of school administration and instruction are resistant to change.

📖 *Innovation in the Knowledge Economy: Implications for Education and Learning*, 2004, Chapter 2

The growing focus on educational outcomes has resulted in both an explosion of evidence of different kinds and a policy thirst for the results of educational research: There is a mounting preoccupation with what happens as a result of educational investments and participation, rather than the primary focus being on these inputs. Outcomes cover not only course completion and qualifications, but also skills and competences (as with the PISA surveys), access to and success in the labour market, and wider social outcomes, such as health and citizenship, attributable to education. There has been a huge expansion of evidence resulting from the growing volume of testing and assessment activities. As policy increasingly focuses on what education actually delivers, so is there interest in the information coming from research, but we know too little about how this evidence is used and whether it is used effectively.

📖 *Evidence in Education: Linking Research and Policy*, 2007, Chapter 1

Too much educational decision making is preoccupied by the short term: Today's world is increasingly complex and uncertain, with a growing number of stakeholders making new demands on education. Yet, so much of education is still determined by short-term thinking – preoccupation with pressing immediate problems or simply seeking more efficient ways of maintaining established practice. Neglect of the long term is increasingly problematic in meeting the challenges of complexity and change. Futures thinking can stimulate reflection on the major changes taking place in education and its wider environment. It helps to clarify visions of what schooling should be and how to get there, and the undesirable futures to avoid. As well as clarifying values and options, it provides tools to engage in strategic dialogue.

📖 *Think Scenarios, Rethink Education*, 2006, Foreword and Part 2

Box 8.1. **Innovation in Education**

Innovation in education has attracted increasing attention. The US stimulus package has for example allocated USD 650 million of its USD 5 billion investment in school reform to a new Investing in Innovation Fund (i3). The fund supports local efforts to start or expand research-based innovative programmes to help close the achievement gap and improve outcomes for students. In 2009, the Netherlands also published an explicit Social Innovation Agenda for Education, and Hungary is reviewing its educational innovation system. However, most countries still need to turn their implicit educational innovation strategies into explicit ones.

…

In recent years, greater emphasis has been placed on the development and use of evidence in teaching. Educational research based on methodologies for measuring causal impacts has grown and increased the body of available knowledge. New links with neuroscience are also promising as they allow better understanding and diagnosis of certain learning difficulties. The enhancement of educational research will remain a serious challenge in the years to come, and developing the necessary evidence will require further work.

New educational products, resources and teaching methods are another source of innovation in education. ICT has led to the development of resources, such as learning management systems and other information systems and diagnostic tools. While the impact of these resources on the quality or cost-efficiency of education is still to be assessed, the increasing involvement of businesses in the production of new educational resources or models opens new avenues. In many cases, however, this market is limited by insufficient demand from schools.

Some education systems are establishing a new generation of sophisticated information infrastructures, such as longitudinal information systems which give rapid feedback to teachers, parents and other stakeholders. In addition to potentially changing the culture of the teaching profession, these systems may remove a key barrier to educational innovation: the difficulty of demonstrating the positive value of educational innovations. As long as innovation cannot be clearly linked to better achievement of educational objectives (learning outcomes, equity, access, cost-efficiency), the innovation process will be slowed by a lack of demand or avoidance of what may simply appear to be another educational fad.

To develop new models of educational delivery, most governments encourage experimentation by the public school systems or fund access to private schools offering alternative schooling models. Innovation and experimentation funds, as well as innovation prizes and rewards, give stakeholders incentives to develop innovative methods. Some countries have used market mechanisms within their public education systems in order to facilitate innovation (*e.g.* charter schools). These mechanisms have generated organisational and marketing innovation. While it is less clear that they have led to innovation in the core business of education, they have contributed to the dissemination of alternative learning environments (collaborative learning, bilingual schools, computer schools, etc). New models of higher education institutions are also appearing in OECD countries, based on storytelling curricula, engineering projects or purely online learning.

User-driven innovation has also become more prominent in the past decade in education owing to the Internet. A number of higher education institutions now offer open educational resources. In addition, wikis and repositories of different types of educational resources are available to students and teachers worldwide.

Insufficient evidence that an educational innovation represents a significant improvement over traditional or mainstream practices hinders the demand for innovation: students, parents or teachers tend to prefer well-known methods rather than experiment with new ones. Potential innovators also lack incentives to innovate in view of the lack of a clear market for their new products or models. As a result, the use and development of innovations remains fragmented. This is why measurement and evaluation of educational change and innovation will be essential to unleash innovation in education.

Source: OECD (2010), *The OECD Innovation Strategy: Getting a Head Start on Tomorrow,* OECD Publishing.

POLICY DIRECTIONS

The OECD's horizontal "Innovation Strategy", in considering how people can be empowered to innovate, concluded with a set of "policy principles" about education and training systems, and innovative workplaces. These tend to parallel closely more general conclusions about education and training policy:

- **Equip people with skills for innovation:** Ensure that education and training systems are adaptable, and can accommodate the changing nature of innovation and the demands of the future. Curricula and pedagogies should develop the capacity to learn new skills and take full advantage of information and communications technologies.

- **Improve educational outcomes:** A considerable share of children still do not complete upper secondary education or leave schools with poor literacy and numeracy skills. While virtually all young people in OECD countries have access to at least 12 years of formal education, mechanisms are needed to ensure that solid educational foundations are universal.

- **Continue to reform tertiary education systems:** Public authorities should enable tertiary education institutions to become catalysts for innovation, notably in their local and regional settings. While the steering role should be reserved for government, institutions should have considerable room for manoeuvre. The tertiary sector also needs to retain sufficient diversity to respond to future needs in the innovation system.

- **Connect vocational education and training to the world of work:** This requires a good balance between occupationally-specific skills that meet employers' needs and generic transferable skills that equip graduates for lifelong learning and mobility.

- **Enable women to play a larger role in the innovation process:** Although female educational attainment tends now to outstrip that of men, the tax and benefit systems, and workplace practices and childcare are key to fuller engagement by women in the labour force and innovation.

- **Support international mobility:** Policies should support knowledge flows and the creation of enduring linkages across countries. Migration regimes for the highly skilled should: be efficient, transparent and simple; enable short-term/circular movements; and support connections to nationals abroad.

- **Foster innovative workplaces:** Employee involvement and effective labour management help to foster creativity and innovation, and employment policies should encourage efficient organisational change. Learning and interaction within firms are key to their innovation performance; governments may also shape national institutions to support higher levels of employee learning and training.

📖 *The OECD Innovation Strategy: Getting a Head Start on Tomorrow*, 2010, Chapter 3

Effective decision making means to be informed as far as possible by evidence, with educational professionals working in a "knowledge-rich" environment: There is need for better links between educational research, policy and practice, and for further progress towards making education a knowledge-rich profession. Greater access to web-based information goes hand-in-hand with less quality control, alongside a shift in most OECD countries towards more decentralised decision making in education. Given greater information, less quality control, a more informed public and a greater diversity of policy makers, the need for clear, reliable and easily available evidence on which to base decisions has become more important than ever before, as has the need to find mechanisms to obtain reliable answers to pressing policy questions.

📖 *Evidence in Education: Linking Research and Policy*, 2007, Chapter 1

Create and encourage knowledge brokerage in education systems: Brokerage agencies are increasingly important to encourage dialogue between policy makers, researchers and educators, and to build capacity to evaluate what does and does not work. An important first step is to create a database of quality research on key topics of interest to policy makers, and to provide clear goals for conducting and evaluating educational research. A key component of these brokerage agencies is the transparent exchange of findings with their methodologies clearly defined, with commitment to update and maintain state-of-the-art syntheses on core topics. And, all centres should seek to disseminate to as wide an audience as possible in order to effect both top-down and bottom-up change.

📖 *Evidence in Education: Linking Research and Policy*, 2007, Chapter 1

Governments can foster investments and stimulate the production of digital learning resources (DLRs) both by commercial companies/publishers and users by:

- **Offering seed money, supplemented with development and transition funds:** The production of DLRs can be stimulated by offering public tender seed money to publishers, supplemented by development project funding and support to help keep innovations afloat once the initial project funding has ended.

- **Promoting co-operation between public and private players for DLR development:** Governments can encourage companies to develop corporate social responsibility programmes and to increase co-operation with public authorities in education. Schools and local educational authorities will need guidelines on how best to approach such co-operation.

📖 *Beyond Textbooks: Digital Learning Resources as Systemic Innovation in the Nordic Countries*, 2009, Chapter 7

A systemic approach to innovation in VET is urgent: Precisely in times of economic crisis, innovation is increasingly a key factor, not only to economic growth, but also to social welfare. A recent study of systemic innovation in the VET sector suggested the following guiding policy principles:

- Develop a systemic approach to innovation in VET as a guiding principle for innovation-related policies.
- Promote a continuous and evidence-informed dialogue about innovation with the VET stakeholders.
- Build a well-organised, formalised, easy to access, and updated knowledge base about VET as a prerequisite for successfully internalising the benefits of innovation.
- Supplement investments in VET innovations with the necessary efforts in monitoring and evaluation.
- Support relevant research on VET according to national priorities and link these efforts to innovation.

📖 *Working Out Change: Systemic Innovation in Vocational Education and Training*, 2009, Chapter 10

Create an effective interface between innovation and higher education systems: Such an interface is essential in order to reap the benefits from public and private investments in research, and to ensure the vitality and quality of higher education systems. Directions for creating such an interface include:

- **Improve knowledge diffusion rather than commercialisation via stronger intellectual property rights (IPRs):** Innovation is not only a discovery process to then be commercialised but R&D is often problem solving along a pathway of innovation. The diffusion capabilities and support activities of tertiary education institutions may thus be as important as discovery processes, and policy should consider methods and instruments to promote them.

- **Improve and widen channels of interaction, and encourage inter-institutional collaboration:** Linkages between the tertiary education sector and other actors in the research and innovation system, such as firms and public research organisations, need to be actively developed to ensure

effective knowledge diffusion. When programmes are designed, they need to consider in particular the engagement of small- and medium-sized enterprises from all technological sectors as they tend to be under-represented in such collaborations.

- **Foster mobility across the research and innovation system:** Inter-sectoral mobility is one of the main vehicles for knowledge diffusion; mobility between firms, tertiary education institutions and public research organisation should be actively promoted.

📖 *Tertiary Education for the Knowledge Society: Volume 2*, 2008, Chapter 7

References

OECD (2004), *Innovation in the Knowledge Economy: Implications for Education and Learning*, OECD Publishing.

OECD (2006), *Think Scenarios, Rethink Education*, OECD Publishing.

OECD (2007), *Evidence in Education: Linking Research to Policy*, OECD Publishing.

OECD (2008), *Tertiary Education for the Knowledge Society: Volume 2*, OECD Publishing.

OECD (2009), *Beyond Textbooks: Digital Learning Resources as Systemic Innovation in the Nordic Countries*, OECD Publishing.

OECD (2009), *Working Out Change: Systemic Innovation in Vocational Education and Training*, OECD Publishing.

OECD (2010), *The OECD Innovation Strategy: Getting a Head Start on Tomorrow*, OECD Publishing.

OECD PUBLICATIONS, 2, rue André-Pascal, 75775 PARIS CEDEX 16
PRINTED IN FRANCE
(96 2010 11 1P) ISBN 978-92-64-09061-3 – No. 57571 2010

Printed in Great Britain
by Amazon.co.uk, Ltd.,
Marston Gate.

Education Today 2010

THE OECD PERSPECTIVE

OECD

ORGANISATION FOR ECONOMIC CO-OPERATION AND DEVELOPMENT

The OECD is a unique forum where governments work together to address the economic, social and environmental challenges of globalisation. The OECD is also at the forefront of efforts to understand and to help governments respond to new developments and concerns, such as corporate governance, the information economy and the challenges of an ageing population. The Organisation provides a setting where governments can compare policy experiences, seek answers to common problems, identify good practice and work to co-ordinate domestic and international policies.

The OECD member countries are: Australia, Austria, Belgium, Canada, Chile, the Czech Republic, Denmark, Finland, France, Germany, Greece, Hungary, Iceland, Ireland, Israel, Italy, Japan, Korea, Luxembourg, Mexico, the Netherlands, New Zealand, Norway, Poland, Portugal, the Slovak Republic, Spain, Sweden, Switzerland, Turkey, the United Kingdom and the United States. The Commission of the European Communities takes part in the work of the OECD.

OECD Publishing disseminates widely the results of the Organisation's statistics gathering and research on economic, social and environmental issues, as well as the conventions, guidelines and standards agreed by its members.

This work is published on the responsibility of the Secretary-General of the OECD. The opinions expressed and arguments employed herein do not necessarily reflect the official views of the Organisation or of the governments of its member countries.

ISBN 978-92-64-09061-3 (print)
ISBN 978-92-64-09062-0 (PDF)

Also available in French: *L'éducation aujourd'hui 2010 : La perspective de l'OCDE*

Photo credits:
Stocklib Image Bank © Cathy Yeulet
Stocklib Image Bank © Nailia Schwarz
Fotolio.com © Elenathewise
Fotolio.com © Franz Pfluegl
Fotolio.com © Kadal
Fotolio.com © pressmaster
Fotolio.com © Tan Kian Khoon

Corrigenda to OECD publications may be found on line at: *www.oecd.org/publishing/corrigenda*.